# UNBROKEN

## TRIALS TO TRIUMPH: THE MAKING OF A COMMUNITY LEADER

*Rommel Sergio*

INDIA • SINGAPORE • MALAYSIA

ISBN 979-8-88783-592-1

Before you create a difference in the world,

you must first learn how to be compassionate.

The power to give is the ability to be kind.

# Contents

# Preface

We are all caught up in a vicious trap, and yet, it is a trap of our own making. We feel that this life, and thus community leadership, is difficult. Our human frailties consciously make us feel limited, imperfect, and inadequate.

Moreover, we allow others to define who we are. With little appreciation of ourselves, seeking others' perception of us and acceptance from them, we find ourselves wounded. We tend to doubt our true selves and value. We allow negativity to affect our level of effectiveness both as individuals and as community leaders.

The power to give without expecting anything in return, and the ability to influence others through sustained commitment and leadership, are the major themes arising from any community engagement. Inspired by my first best-selling book *Managing Cases: Thriving Organizations in the New Normal,* this second book recounts my personal, painstaking journey of toil, trials, and triumphs over the past three decades toward being a community leader.

In the long run, self-discovery and growth, no matter how painful they are, combine to create a powerful force that contributes to the betterment of ourselves and thus of the communities we serve.

As we equip ourselves with our life lessons, our own stories, and our competencies, we inspire others by continuously igniting the passion to serve and kindling the desire to look for what is true and what is right and what is best in humanity.

Yes, we are imperfect. We are disheartened, disappointed, bruised. We struggle to overcome the seemingly insurmountable waves of struggle and adversity.

But, dear Reader, we are Unbroken.

And Unbroken we shall remain.

# Acknowledgments

The freedom to stand and remain Unbroken is possible only through the grace, enlightenment, and providence of the Almighty God.

To my parents, Romeo and Florentina, for the gift of life, who, in their own ways, encouraged life lessons and sacrifices;

My family – Cristina, Raymund, Jonas, Mhel, and Adler for their unconditional love and for inspiring the Unbroken Team to move forward;

To the Young Mission Apostles, through Tet and Leo, for making me realize the value of community service and selfless devotion to community work;

To the great community leaders who may have been bruised and in pain, who grappled with untold misery and loss, but were courageous and determined to journey towards wholeness and community leadership, inspiring others to join them in their quest for self-discovery and service to humanity;

To the currently aspiring community leaders, and, therefore, catalysts of change;

To all the educators who instilled in me the values of unconditional giving and compassion;

To Prof. Dr. Karim Chelli, Canadian University Dubai President and Vice Chancellor, for his transformational leadership worth emulating;

To Dabarkads Jenny, Dr. Rebecca, Consul General Ferdie, Mariecar, Emy, and Maynard who were with me in most of my community work and for inspiring me to do more for others;

To Jonas, Troi Santos of CNN, and the Illustrado team, for their unbending support in bringing to life a thousand words through their photos;

To Dr. Ruthmita H. Rozul and Dr. Kathy O'Sullivan, for their invaluable insights, guidance, and technical skills that led to the fruition of this writing project;

This book is dedicated to all of you.

# Introduction

We are a part of a community that cares. We are never alone. Life may be challenging but it is still beautiful and ever-changing. We must constantly move to its rhythm. We can either choose to be left behind and stay in the dark, or we can decide to take action and lead others along the path of enlightenment and happiness.

We are meant to do extraordinary things - if we will recognize the reality that we have all, each and every one of us, been endowed with potential. We must embrace all available opportunities, challenge ourselves, and allow ourselves to be empowered.

Just like many individuals who must struggle to survive at a very early stage in their lives, I knew that there was a bumpy road ahead (and "bumpy" was an understatement!) towards my quest for self-actualization. But I knew, too, that through an inherent power, I could discover my innermost strengths, forces that were greater than me, that would allow me to emerge from adversities bowed but unscathed, healed and made whole, so that I could inspire others to lead and serve communities as well.

This book unveils my toil, trials, and triumphs as a community leader during the pre- and post-COVID eras. Important lessons related to self-discovery, recognizing one's competencies, and responding to community needs are scenarios of toil and trials that have been outlined and discussed at length.

At the end of each chapter is a Reflections section that asks the reader to recount life lessons, takeaways, and application points.

Triumphs do not happen at the touch of a button. They are brought about by possessing salient values of self-compassion, mindfulness, dependability, optimism, ethical leadership, and the power to appreciate small and extraordinary wins that can spindle happiness even to greater heights.

I beseech the readers of this book to learn and apply the lessons found herein. Only in self-less giving and engagement with humanity can we find our true purpose.

We are all destined to do extraordinary things. Each of us must start our personal voyage of discovery as an individual.

Dear Reader, let your community leadership journey begin and your own Unbroken stories be told.

Chapter 1

# A Life-Changing Journey

”

**We don't develop courage by being happy every day. We develop it by surviving difficult times and challenging adversity.**

*Barbara De Angelis*

Reader, let me tell you a story.

I have always lived up to the following truths:

Knowing what's out there in the world is essential to the health and wellness of one's collected affairs. However, knowing oneself is even more fundamental, life-changing, and cathartic.

My thoughts ran along these very lines, haltingly pounding away on a manual Brother typewriter one stormy night many, many years ago. I was in my third year at university, editor-in-chief of the student publication, and I was struggling – struggling with writer's block. At that time, I was juggling responsibilities at home – I was the eldest in the family of four siblings - and those activities at the university. I was also a student leader and was involved in decision-making processes on matters affecting student wellbeing, all of which were time-consuming. But I am getting ahead of my story.

I experienced trauma in my elementary days. My grade school teachers and classmates saw me as a very introverted type of person, in terms of my refraining from taking on any role that would place me as the center of attention.

I experienced trauma in my elementary days. My grade school teachers and classmates saw me as a very introverted type of person, in terms of my refraining from taking on any role that would place me as the center of attention.

"Swallowed your tongue again?" someone would ask sarcastically.

"Oh, yes! As usual!" Someone would answer for me. Many would laugh in chorus. I felt bullied. It continued until I finished grade school.

That would be the way other people would perceive me as being quiet, reserved, meek, tight-lipped, uncommunicative, and passive. would sooner die than speak in public. The reason for this was the paralyzing combination of shyness and insecurities that I would feel each time I was made to answer a question or state my point of view. My classmates would never hear me utter anything off the top of my head! The daily class recitation was the most grueling part of my elementary school days and teachers had a difficult time assessing my abilities because of this lack of willingness to say anything at all – before, during, and even after classes.

I would barely speak a word. I would babble incoherently, afraid to stay long at an utterance since there was a very real possibility that I would be asked to repeat, and when that scenario would happen, I would simply remain quiet and turn away. The embarrassment and pain of ridicule were acute and lasting, and people rarely paid attention to me and to what I would have to say.

Being labeled as the quiet one, the 'passive' one, made me the butt of the grownups' jokes, and also of the other students' pointing fingers at each other because no one wanted to include me as a member of their group, especially in anything involving presenting to an audience.

I was told that I was passive, being too quiet, uncaring even, was a manifestation of weakness. That was what the grownups said. Terms such as weak, feeble, wimpy, passive, and incompetent were used to describe me, among others. I knew I had something important to say but I could not verbalize my ideas and did not have the strength to do it. People asked me, implored me, told me, commanded me to talk and express what was going on in that head of mine because the environment and society demanded it, they said. I knew I had ideas running amok in my head ('active inside'), knew I was conscious of what was happening around me, and I wanted some sort of consistency between being active inside and also being active outside. I wanted to integrate the outside with the inside, which I believed, represented the real me, my true self and identity. I simply could not form my thoughts and say my words out loud. I knew I had to do something but I did not have the power to do it. I felt that I did not have the right tools to form my words. I did discern that I could contribute, be somebody, make a difference, do extraordinary things, change the world even, but, alas, I simply did not know how to begin.

> My teacher threw a chalk eraser at me. The chalk eraser landed squarely on my face. I was too humiliated to react! I felt very small. While crying, that scene of wiping away chalk dust from my face while all the other students were staring at me created the torturous image that would haunt me for years afterwards.

I would worry my family, my parents especially, and my too quiet behavior caused them to explain away to people all sorts of imagined scenarios about why I was not talking. The environment that I was in looked askance at me. Though people did not publicly censure me, I behaved far from the usual norm set by society and I was thus looked upon with disfavor and distrust.

I remember quite well that day when I was in the fourth grade. It was a particularly horrid day when one of my teachers decided that she was not in the mood to wait on a student who would not talk! I was even more quiet than usual that day and was not participating in the discussion at all. So, she decided that she would not put up with me this time, that she would not motivate me to talk any longer, that it was high time she showed the class who was boss! She threw a chalk eraser at me! (It was the time when green chalkboards and chalk erasers were still very much in use!) The chalk eraser landed squarely on my face! I was too humiliated to react! I felt very small. I simply got my Boy Scout handkerchief out of my pocket and slowly wiped the chalk dust from my face. That scene of wiping away while crying chalk dust from my face while all the other students were staring at me created the torturous image that would haunt me for years afterwards.

On that day, I was a child in the fourth grade, yet I determined that I would be even quieter, even more passive. That decision made my elementary days sad and messy, and my future doubly uncertain.

## Baras, Rizal

Baras, Rizal is a fourth-class municipality situated in the province of Rizal in the Philippines. It is my birthplace and the home of my people. It is the smallest place geographically among the eleven towns of the province. Founded in 1595 by Franciscan missionaries, Baras' main claims to fame were the establishment of a military camp by the revolutionary Katipunan (a Filipino revolutionary society plotting against their colonisers) in 1895 that drove the Spaniards away and began the municipal township, and the Diocesan Shrine and Parish of Saint Joseph which was founded in 1682 and which enshrines the miraculous venerated image of San Jose de Baras.

I digressed a little to this town of Baras to show the kind of environment which taught me my first values. When I was young, the town was very old, and the ways of living and thinking were not forward-looking, the way people would sometimes cling to learned mores and principles and never leave them, even if these norms were detrimental to the health and wellbeing of its citizens. Much has changed now, but that was then, during my boyhood.

In that closely-knit environment, my family loved me profoundly, yet, I was not taught to overcome my speech difficulties, nor how to be confident. It was not because they did not care, but, rather, that they did not know how. Their knowledge was limited and they were at a loss as to the right course of action to take to help me talk. More importantly, neither was I taught to dream, to dream big, to transcend limits, to make a difference, to contribute, to become extraordinary. Instead, my end goal in life was to follow the crowd, to live simply, to just 'finish my studies'. The grownups merely told me what they had been told themselves when they were young! There was therefore no escaping the troubles that I have had during my elementary years!

So life for me during my elementary days was rather more of a challenge than a blessing. How I waited impatiently for these days to end and my high school days to begin!

My parents did not want me to go to 'some big university', probably because of our socioeconomic status. We were very poor. Another reason was the usual state of mind of people in the province - that finishing education was indeed important, but we could not afford it so we needed to make the most out of what the public school and university had to offer. By their standards, the local college in the next town would do just fine. After college, they said that I should get a job and earn for myself and the family. This, they declared, was the fundamental approach to becoming successful in life. "Secure your education, then the rest will follow," they advised me.

## Transformation

High school was a transformative environment for me. It was the place where I decided that, if I were to survive, a change of direction and behavior was warranted. I needed to alter my being passive on the outside, and active *only* on the inside! I must be active on *both* sides – in and out! I thought that setting up changes in my environment would make it easier to do what was right without having to think about staying motivated. I realized that a shift from one kind of environment to another would solve my speech problem. A lasting change would soon happen!

I went to attend in the next town a state university that also offered secondary education. I went on to become a high school 'Star Scholar', awarded through the provincial governor's foundation. I completed my secondary and tertiary education at this state university. This new environment changed my perspective because, most importantly, I was not judged, bullied, or made fun of! Unbelievably, my English teacher told me that I had what it took not only to talk out loud and coherently but also to compete. She motivated me. She trained me. She beat me. She pummeled the shyness and awkwardness and hesitation and fear out of me. That humiliating process that had been in train for years suddenly stopped. My speaking skills, my abilities to engage orally with people, my self-confidence – went from zero in elementary days to hero in the university! I shifted gears in university by joining extemporaneous speaking contests and debates. Who would have ever guessed? That a young boy who could not utter the proper words in elementary would rise to become an extemporaneous speaker and a debater? That someone from a small municipal town would be known at a bigger, grander venue? Like Gideon of the Bible, his answer to the angel of the Lord when he was summoned to deliver Israel from the hands of the Midians, said, "Pray, Lord, how can I deliver Israel? Behold, my clan is the weakest in Manasseh, and I am the least in my family" (Judges 6:15-16). The Lord said to him, "I will be with you."

And the Lord was with me, too.

## A Teacher in the Making

I decided that teaching would be the best choice of a profession for me because I would have the power to influence. And for me to do that, I would need to know the world, the whole gamut of what was there to know (I thought of politics and government, mainly, and anything related to the environment). I asked myself, "What's happening in the world? Everything's a construct, an idea, a knowledge transfer, a skill transfer, competency building in general." And I wanted to become part of all these things! Perhaps all at the same time! Finally, I could express the most important things I had bottled up inside. To my mind, I could now do extraordinary things, achieve my long-cherished dream – to be successful in whatever I set my heart and mind on.

> **When the right time came, because of another teacher, that boy, now a man, set out in his heart to make a difference in this world. It's quite a marvel that he, too, ended up being a teacher just like the eraser-throwing instructor (who he promised he would never imitate).**

Even at a young age, I knew I loved learning and processing information very quickly in my mind, even though I found the information difficult to express. I knew what excellence meant, what being academically gifted was all about. I had things figured out in my mind. I could process things simultaneously in my mind with speed, clarity, and correctness. Again, my only concern was my environment, which to me, was not helping at all in terms of my self-expression and in overcoming my speech difficulties.

That English teacher gave me an opportunity that perhaps comes along only once in a lifetime. Suddenly, things shifted for me. I began to see newness and freshness, began to see different perspectives. My environment began to support me. I started studying with teachers who said that I could do it, that I had the potential in me to do it. I began to be transformed. This transformation not only surprised me for one, but it also surprised my loved ones, my parents, my family, because they knew how passive I was, how introverted I was. I began bringing home certificates after certificates – for winning different speaking contests and for academic merit. It was not an easy journey. This feat of bringing home awards and laurels began with a little boy, just ten years of age, who was afraid to talk and had a chalk eraser thrown at him by a teacher in front of the whole class. However, when the right time came, because of *another* teacher, that boy, now a man, set out in his heart to make a difference in this world. It's quite a marvel that he, too, ended up being a teacher just like the eraser-throwing instructor (who he promised he would never imitate)!

Imagine the influence of teachers! Imagine the sort of influence my teachers had on me! A smile, a nod of the head, a pat on the back, an affirmation, an insistence, a declaration – and my life took on an unbelievable, unimaginable course that would eventually bring honor and recognition to my fellowmen and to my country – that would make the name 'Filipino' a byword for excellence, dedication, determination, strength, and resilience.

That was an achievement and that, in itself, is already a milestone.

## Reflections

Key Insights: Draw from this Chapter your major takeaways.

1. ______________________________

______________________________

______________________________

2. ______________________________

______________________________

______________________________

3. ______________________________

______________________________

______________________________

Recount events in your life related to the Key Insights.

1. ______________________________

______________________________

______________________________

2. ______________________________

______________________________

______________________________

3. ______________________________

______________________________

______________________________

How can these Key Insights guide you and prepare you for life's present and future challenges?

1. ______________________________________________

______________________________________________

______________________________________________

2. ______________________________________________

______________________________________________

______________________________________________

3. ______________________________________________

______________________________________________

______________________________________________

# Chapter 2

## Tapped, Yet Untapped

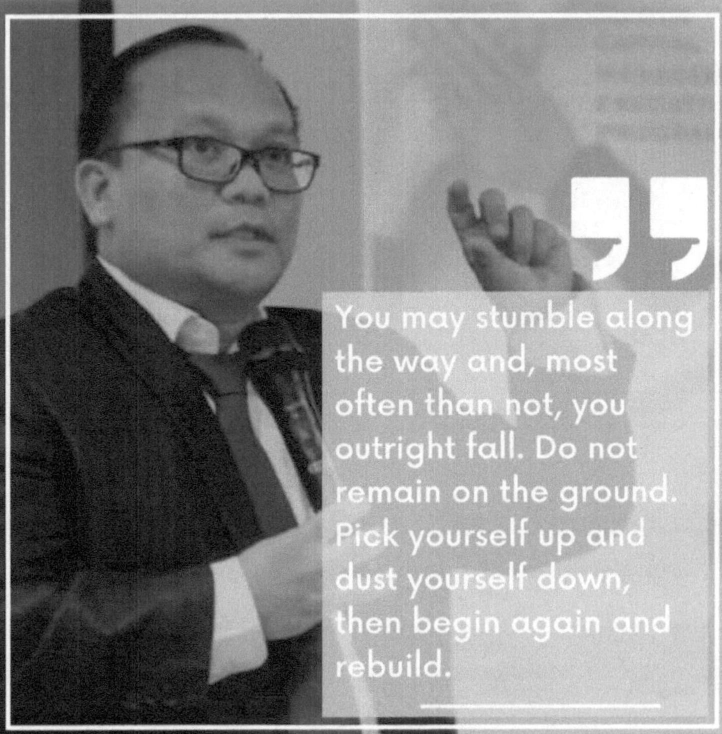

**Let the past sleep,**
*but let it sleep in the bosom of Christ.*

**Leave the irreparable past in His hands,**
*and step out into the irresistible future with Him.*

Oswald Chambers

"The apple never falls far from the tree," or so they say. This idea expresses that a child inevitably shares characteristics with the parent, whether the child wants such traits or not.

I was raised by a very strict father. He was a member of the Scout Rangers, a tough unit of the Philippine Army. Having specialized in raids, ambushes, sabotage, close-quarter combats, anti-guerrilla jungle warfare, and urban combat, no wonder I grew up the way I did, with my father bringing these influences home with him. From home to the front, then back home. A psychological study of the soldier at this juncture of my narrative would not be amiss since I believed that my father had suffered under the peculiar physical, emotional, and mental strain of being a soldier defending his country, therefore exhibiting certain qualities that were not his own.

What was his motto at home? The reader may wonder about this. It was "never ask, just obey". It seemed strange not to be able to speak one's mind at home but to merely shut up and follow orders. Perhaps this overly tight control of his family and my seeing the military uniform everywhere in the house, even if my father was not present, probably started my being uncommunicative about my feelings, my being quiet, reserved, and passive on the outside. Undiagnosed by a medical practitioner back then, this is what I surmise now as to the cause of all my troubles at a young age. No, the members of my family formed no real army – but we were a uniformed crowd nonetheless. I believe that my mother and each of my siblings experienced trauma that would perhaps be labeled similar to mine, but their stories are theirs to tell. They will perhaps speak their own truth one day.

My father's goal was to get his children into what he considered as the proper frame of mind and give them the *esprit de corps* which is essential for a successful life. Finishing one's education was the key to a rewarding existence. We were not allowed to think about the affairs of life, only do household chores and finish our studies, and it was the rule of the house never to contradict him. He alone possessed common sense.

Required to be up and about at three o'clock in the morning every day, even at weekends, my routine would be similar to this: groping in the dark, I would first light a tiny *lampara* using worn-out matches from the stove, while the smell of kerosene filled our tiny room-of-a-house, careful not to put my face too close to the lamp, otherwise, my nose would be filled with the black soot emanating from the flames. I would then prepare a cup of coffee from a little three-in-one sachet using a *puswelo* (mug), mixing with it a little brown sugar to remove the bitter taste. I would also eat a little brown bread, the *pandesal* – a leftover from yesterday's afternoon snack, dipping the *pandesal* into the mug of coffee for that extra flavor. After this meager breakfast, I would then take the little *bolo* (a large single-edged knife used in the Philippines) hanging from the nail on the *dingding* (our wall was constructed using native materials), then make my way gingerly out of the house in semi-darkness with the gas lamp held over my head, careful not to trip over some branch or twig lying on the ground and risk breaking the gas lamp. After walking for about one hour, I would find myself in the nearby forest where *ipil-ipil*, *madre de cacao*, and *nipa* trees grew in profusion. I would put down the lamp and with the use of the little *bolo*, chop down the low branches of these trees but refrain from hurting the roots, leaving the trees alive. Afterwards, I would try to cut the wood in similar lengths for easy carrying, then gather and bundle them up using the strong and long *nipa* leaves, carry the bundles back home (as many bundles as my little shoulders could carry) then sell them to neighbors when day began to break. In about three hours, I would have completed the task of getting myself to the forest, gathering firewood, walking back home, and selling the bundles in nearby houses before getting dressed up and bracing myself for a long day at school. Houses that were located far away would have to wait for their firewood until I could get home from school in the afternoon. A bundle would earn the family P1.00. I could sell as many as ten bundles a day, enough to replenish the stock of our little *sari-sari* (convenience) store.

Very few neighbors had electricity installed in their houses had gas ranges in their kitchens, so the firewood (my firewood!) was always a life-saver! I would first go from house to house collecting orders in the afternoon or early evening after coming home from school, and then deliver the following day. In some ways, yes, it was simple, and yet it gave us a more thorough understanding of the complexities of the world than most of the smartphone generation have today, and since the community was small, it was cash-strapped.

My family ran a little *sari-sari* store, the neighborhood convenience store, one of many which dot the streets. It sold the most basic of goods, i.e. rice, coffee, milk, salt, sugar, cooking oil, fish sauce, vinegar, sardines, noodles, some candies, as well as long sachets of shampoos, conditioners, and tubes of toothpaste all hanging from the ceiling like a colorful Christmas tree! The neighbors could only afford to buy *tingi*, or retail, since the whole package would cost more than the units.

We did not have any signage on our store, like "Florentina's Store" or a "Sergio's Store", because we could not afford the price of the tarpaulin. A soft-drink company would have had put up one for us but we would have had to order cases of soft-drinks from them first. We could not afford to do that either since we did not have any refrigerator for storing the bottles. In addition, we would not be able to afford the increase in the electric bill that would come with owning a refrigerator.

> **When the right time came, because of another teacher, that boy, now a man, set out in his heart to make a difference in this world. It's quite a marvel that he, too, ended up being a teacher just like the eraser-throwing instructor (who he promised he would never imitate).**

My mother allowed credit purchases from her *suki* (repeat customers known to her), much to the dismay of my father because very little is earned from such customers.

She kept a record of these customers' outstanding balances in one of my old school notebooks and she would demand payments every 15th and 30th of the month. My father, upon seeing the long list of non-paying customers, wrote on a cardboard *Bawal Utang* (No Credit), and he then posted it on the wall of the store. From that time on, no one tried credit with Mother anymore, but some of her *suki* transferred their shopping to another store on another street where credit was allowed.

I had very little play, which is an important part of learning and communication, when I was a child. Most of my childhood was work, work, work. Coupled with my speech difficulties, I could say that my boyhood was not an idyllic childhood.

Thus, the typical travails of my boyhood can be summed up in these words:

*What ultimately makes a man all stems from the misery handed to him.*

However, I had a choice when it came to dealing with this misery. Loathe it or learn from it.

I chose the latter.

So my story continues.

I tend to view high school as one of the most transformative stages in my life. My path to being

**The typical travails of my boyhood can be summed up in these words: What ultimately makes a man all stems from the misery handed to him.**

**However, I had a choice when it came to dealing with this misery. Loathe it or learn from it.**

successful in life was not a straight line. Rather, it had a twist. I was approached by many people during high school, who, upon seeing my potential, tried to persuade me to become more involved with school as a student leader. At first, some teachers invited me to see them in their office. They explained that the school was in a bad way and needed student leaders. Would I consider running for president of the student council? I listened to them talk, nodded my head a couple of times, but did not commit myself. Then a couple who taught arts, music, drafting, and calligraphy in my school also asked me to see them in their office. They invited me to join their church at Baras, the smallest among the towns of Rizal Province in the Philippines. Although I said no to their invitation, this couple became two of the most influential people in my life. I declined their offer because I thought that I would achieve growth in a different place, not in a church. However, this couple – Tet and Leo, remained steadfast in their belief that I should join their church and that I would experience spiritual and personal growth within this church. Finally, I said yes, I would join their organization, the Young Mission Apostles (YMA), as a choir member.

> **My community engagement started with my being part of the church organization which turned out to be a civic one, too. There were always opportunities for collaboration and engagements with the poorest of the poor: the last, the least, the lost.**

Tet was my Drafting teacher in high school. Patient, competent, and genuinely interested in encouraging me, she was inspirational. She told me that we could serve our community together. The desire to win the praise of friends, and of the community, and the sense of the heroic, were very keen in me, and I said yes to her. She has been a great mentor, a comrade, a true friend, and is now a colleague, one of the greatest influencers on my personal and professional growth.

> **I was born poor. I grew up in a household, in an impoverished community. I wore shabby clothes as a child, sold firewood, looked after the store, and worked and played with other underprivileged children. I needed very little but contented with life.**

This part of my life now was characterized by a number of progress milestones in quick succession: I was no longer a passive observer. I evolved from being reserved, quiet and self-contained into being an active community member. In joining this church, I took control of my speaking ability and I started to play an unusually important role in leadership. Finally, I started to feel that I could be one of the crowd or the common people" with "a member of a group, a community. I could now talk, express myself clearly, and I could make people pause what they were doing and listen to me. I could make them change their minds and re-evaluate.

Although I had wanted for some time to have people listen to what I wanted – no, needed - to say, I had no audience. Now, I was a contender for more important posts, people started to notice my ability to connect and share my talent and my audience kept getting bigger every day as I gained confidence and became better at communicating to an audience.

The memory of my humble beginnings was always preying on my mind so my ego was constantly checked to resist unwelcome and unchristian suggestions. And I was definitely on the road to success! But, alas, I started on this road with caution. People warned me against success going to my head, that I did not have to dream big because *that* would only lead to trouble and disappointment.

> **Working and serving the poor at this point in my life would not be new to me. Therefore, this chance of serving the needy and the destitute in their hour of greatest need was an opportunity that I welcomed and embraced.**

My answer to these warnings was simple: people took notice of me when I least expected that anyone would, and they tapped the untapped in me. I was approached at several levels and on numerous occasions. They saw my potential, and knew that I could reach a wider audience, given the chance. "Hey, you are being noticed. You are being recognized. You are being selected. You are being designated." And so I owe my life to these individuals who saw me, saw the real me, and therefore took the time to tutor me, teach me, to mold me. They took a chance on me, developing me as a seeker of truth, a campaigner, a community leader. I may be basking in glory right now but I do not want to stand in the light alone. I want the community to have what I have. I want to be able to shake hands, to tap shoulders, to look people in the eye, and let them know that they are not alone, that nobody should be alone. Perhaps opportunities get blocked and doors remain closed. If that happens, I promise to help people *build new doors*! I vow to create new opportunities to make the ordinary become extraordinary. When people help each other, amazing things happen. Nothing can stand against people committed to supporting and helping one another. This has been my big dream and, at this point in my life, I can safely say that I have begun to achieve it.

> Growth does happen because I have set my imagination on it. Imagination is a powerful gauge that creates a potent force. An action is thus created and even though impediments find their way into my sphere, I always seem to find another way around them or through them, so much so that I consider impediments and obstacles not as stumbling blocks, but building blocks.

I'm almost fifty years old now and throughout my adult existence, I've always seen growth as a continuous process. But growth must start somewhere and with that first, single step. I believe that when I close my eyes, will things and scenarios and events into existence, they will. I believe in the power of the human mind. One has to know that the imagined can and will happen and, in my case, it always does. It does not only take a complete belief in oneself but a corresponding push in the right direction. Growth does happen because I have set my imagination on it. Imagination is a powerful gauge that creates an internal force that is eventually converted into a potent force. An action is thus created and even though impediments find their way into my sphere, I always seem to find another way around them or through them, so much so that I consider impediments and obstacles not as stumbling blocks, but building blocks. I gather the stumbling blocks thrown at me, and from this chaos, I try to create new building blocks which will serve as tool for the next endeavor. Yes, I stumble along the way and, more often than not, I fall. However, I do not remain on the ground. I pick myself up, dust myself down, then begin and build again.

After just one year as a member of the YMA, becoming choir leader was transformational. My confidence increased by leaps and bounds and finally, what was happening in my environment tallied with and what I perceived myself to be. And it all started with me saying "yes" to being a member of that church choir. So this started me thinking. Had I not accepted the invitation, I would not have experienced being transformed. Life, I now believe, is serendipity. Sometimes we do not need to actively search for things. They will unexpectedly come and find us.

I had very few friends and those friends I did have were like me, the quiet ones. I only had one friend during my entire elementary years. During high school, I decided to even be choosier with friends. One particular guy, who was very much like me, was the first to decide to join the church choir. After a while, I observed that he started to come out of his shell and be expressive in ways that were astonishing to me. When my beloved mentor came to say to me, "See? Your friend has decided to be a part of the church choir. He has become less shy, and more talkative and friendly. Perhaps you'd want to join the choir, too?", I did. I never regretted that decision. It was one of the most important I have ever made in my life.

My community engagement started with my being part of the church organization which turned out to be a civic one, too. There were always opportunities for collaboration and engagements with the poorest of the poor: the last, the least, the lost. I was born poor. I grew up in a household, in an impoverished community. I wore shabby clothes as a child, sold firewood, looked after the store, and worked and played with other underprivileged children. I needed very little. I was used to having just a few coins in my pocket, or none at all. Working and serving the poor at this point in my life would not be new to me. Therefore, this chance of serving the needy and the destitute in their hour of greatest need was an opportunity that I welcomed and embraced. I owed them. My passion to help them was as strong as the very breath in my body.

**My passion to help the needy was as strong as the very breath in my body. There were was no turning back anymore.**

**I was given a gift.**

**I was determined to share it with the world.**

There was no turning back anymore.

I was given a gift.

I was determined to share it with the world.

## Reflections

Key Insights: Draw from this Chapter your major takeaways.

1. ____________________________________________

____________________________________________

____________________________________________

2. ____________________________________________

____________________________________________

____________________________________________

3. ____________________________________________

____________________________________________

____________________________________________

Recount events in your life related to the Key Insights.

1. ____________________________________________

____________________________________________

____________________________________________

2. ____________________________________________

____________________________________________

____________________________________________

3. ____________________________________________

____________________________________________

____________________________________________

How can these Key Insights guide you and prepare you for life's present and future challenges?

1. ______________________________

______________________________

______________________________

2. ______________________________

______________________________

______________________________

3. ______________________________

______________________________

______________________________

# Chapter 3

## The Start of It All

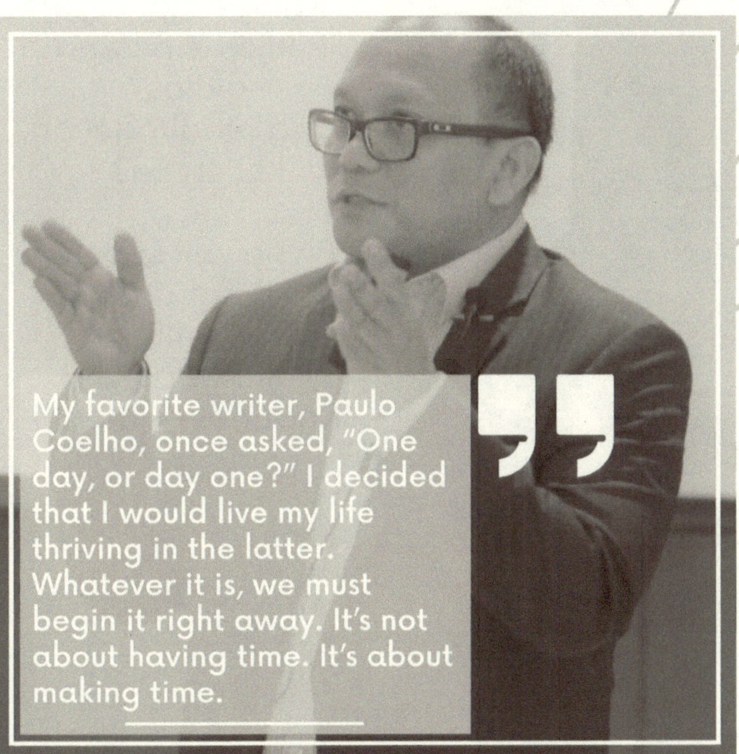

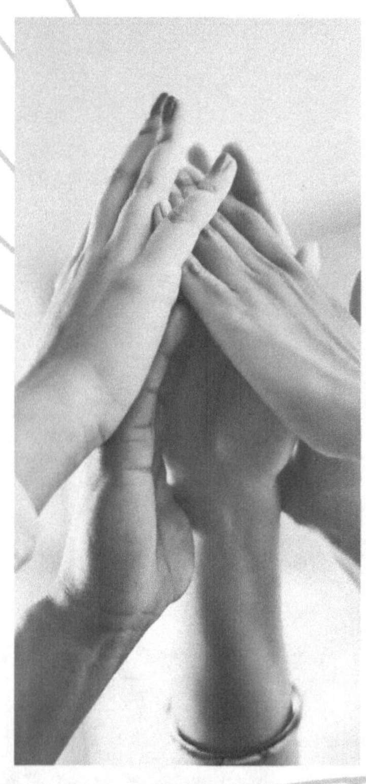

"Kung hindi tayo
kikibo, sino ang
kikibo?
Kung hindi tayo
kikilos, sino ang
kikilos?
Kung hindi ngayon,
kalian pa?"

(Who will speak,
if not us?
Who will act,
if not us?
If not now, when?)

Abraham "Ditto" Sarmiento, Jr.

Growing up, I was always advised to value time, and to start making the best use of it as early as possible, or life would otherwise pass me by.

I can still remember the poem written by Colin Coplin that I learned in high school. The words are forever etched in my mind.

*You've got to start somewhere*
*Now's a good place to start*
*Wait until tomorrow*
*And you may have lost your part.*

*This stage is forever*
*But the chances are few*
*Before you know it*
*They've never heard of you.*

*And you wonder if you'll make it*
*If you'll have no regrets*
*And you're scared of failure*
*And maybe of success.*

*If you don't make a start*
*Then you'll never know*
*If your opening night closes*
*Or is a long-run Broadway show.*

*Children are born*
*They grow and die*
*What they do in between-time*
*Is why they're alive.*

*Got to ride the waves*
*Grab the bull with both horns*
*Before you know it*
*Your life's come, been, and gone…*

The teacher asked me what the poem meant. Deliberately, I said, "I believe that the sooner we start, the better we'll be. Wasting time is dumbing down our society. What is our priority? We should start now. Whatever it is, we must begin it right away. It's not about having time. It's about making time. If we think that time matters, we will make time now." That was the year in high school when I was able to develop my speaking ability and thus was able to explain myself, I believe, fairly well.

I originally thought that this chapter's title would be "Making a Difference" or "If Not Now, When? If Not Me, Who?" but I finally settled on "The Start of It All" which invariably sums up the first two titles.

The existential questions, "Who will speak, if not us? Who will act, if not us? If not now, when?" had always been among my most important guiding philosophies. They had generally shaped my attitude towards work and the way I thought I should live my life. Most importantly, they had defined my struggles between what *was* and what *ought* to be, from being quiet and passive on the inside to being communicative and outgoing. And, dear Reader, you will find out in this chapter more of the hurdles that I had to overcome before I arrived at the place where I am right now.

In the previous chapter, I declared that it took a single (and simple) "yes" to start becoming a community volunteer, then a member, and then a leader, back in my high school days. This was a tremendous improvement from my being seemingly passive on the outside, while being incredibly active on the inside. I must admit to you unashamedly, dear Reader, that I was socially awkward. I could neither convey meaning to an audience nor start a conversation. Then, unbelievably, I made a 360-degree change in the way I presented myself to everyone, especially to those people who knew me very, very well. My friends were shocked! My family was shocked! I was shocked! It was like I had been resurrected, was born again! I was treated with awe and surprise, like a famous movie star coming home for a break and a swim at Baras River!

My favorite writer, Paulo Coelho, once said, "One day, or day one?" I decided that I would live my life thriving in the latter.

Three factors indicated to me that something new was coming.

The first was the incredible opportunity not only to become part of a community but also to lead it. Becoming a community leader initially felt a little daunting, disconcerting, especially with very important personalities as members. But I knew that I had important things to share and sharing these would build my newfound faith and trust in my abilities.

The second factor was the absolutely providential opportunity for me to select a course of specialization in college. In my country, most students enroll in what their families believe they should enroll in, then find suitable jobs afterwards that will support the family and bring food to the table. Since I was the eldest in a brood of four, the expectation would be that the family would tell me about my career path and which program to take. Not all students attending colleges and universities could choose the specializations that they wanted.

I had always been fascinated by psychology as a branch of knowledge, the scientific study of the human mind and its functions, especially those affecting behavior. I needed to fully understand myself, to define my identity, which, then, was still quite hazy and abstract to me. I needed to learn ways to validate my experiences so far and explain the predispositions that I had toward certain people or events. I would be my first patient, I thought.

Taking up psychology strengthened my core belief that I could do things beyond my cognition, much more, indeed, than being a community leader. Being one was not that bad but I knew, deep within me, that my being a leader to communities would simply be an effect, i.e. a consequence, not an end in itself.

I knew that like any other type of art, writing was pain and pleasure at the same time. I could turn into a hermit, for all I knew, or even get burned out. There would be a lot of sacrifice, but it would be worth it in the end.

And so I enrolled in psychology, fully intending to finish it within the required number of years or even less.

The third factor that convinced me that great things were on the horizon was that I won a four-year scholarship at university and, at the same time, maintained this scholarship by keeping my membership in the student publication.

I was always keen on writing and expressing myself through the written word. It was just oral communication that I had so much difficulty with. I had imagined a "life creating fantastical characters from thin air, as you smoke a cigar, and peck away at your typewriter" (NY Book Editors, 2016).

I knew that like any other type of art, writing was pain and pleasure at the same time. I could turn into a hermit, for all I knew, or even get burned out. There would be a lot of sacrifice, but it would be worth it in the end.

I was not simply a writer for the student publication at the university. To further supplement my meager savings, I also sought part-time work as a writer for the Department of Health in Region IV.

I took on multiple roles soon after that: student, student leader, student-writer, a prime mover in my family as the eldest and as a regular earner, a church leader, a community volunteer, a community leader, a *sari-sari* store attendant selling *sago't gulaman* (a local Filipino beverage made of brown sugar, water, gelatin, and tapioca pearls), and a firewood and charcoal seller. These multiple roles awakened in me a sleeping giant, so to speak. I became tremendously busy, full of distracting detail, with plans and designs continually floating in my mind. I was constantly busy with new projects, gripped somehow with the thought that, for many years as an elementary school boy, my time was wasted because I could not speak. A lot of opportunities, perhaps, passed me by because I did not know what to make of them. I did not fully understand the impact that those opportunities could have had on my young life.

Following Colin Coplin, I made very good use of time. I was alive and animated, briskly busy, absolutely thriving. And I started from exactly where I was, from within the confines of my home, school, church, and community.

I say "confines" but I was not held as a prisoner there. I was free as a bird! Free to act as I wanted, free to think what I wanted, free to behave as I wanted, in other words, free to be me. To be my new me! It was a truly exciting time, and I hadn't felt that excited in a long time.

With my days and nights fully taken up with work and study, I had very little time to rest and take a break! Finally, truth be told, and without any apologies, I can now say that the multiple roles cast me into a position of status which brought many, many benefits - both for me and the people around me.

I humbly reveal to you, dear Reader, that the path I begun in life was indeed torturous, rocky, and full of self-doubt, yet it had ultimately led to an intensely gratifying life.

I can say that the biggest push that I had in life was being born poor but never wanting to remain poor. I wanted to escape my condition, to move past it, to move fast the feelings of want and need, and to be able to hope and dream. However, that could hardly be the only thing justifying my 'push'.

*I can say that the biggest push that I had in life was being born poor but never wanting to remain poor.* I wanted to escape my condition, to move past it, to move fast the feelings of want and need, and to be able to hope and dream. However, that could hardly be the only thing justifying my 'push'.

Another reason was that I believe in the uniqueness of every individual. There would never be anyone just like you and me walking around. If only we could clone all the positive traits of humanity into the millions we have on the planet, I think that it would be a far happier place to live in. This is precisely why, in my life now, I give myself (nay, it is more than that), I *empty* myself into the people who need me. I could never turn anyone away. It was built in my nature to be people-centered and community-minded. Although I started my life as a poor boy in Baras, all the difficulties that I experienced made me unique and of valuable, deserving of the respect that people give me now.

One of my secrets to success is consistency. Consistency is key. My quality team had been exactly that – a *quality* team. I tried to do things correctly so that there would not be room for failure. However, if failure resulted, I learned from it, then tried again, learning from the mistake.

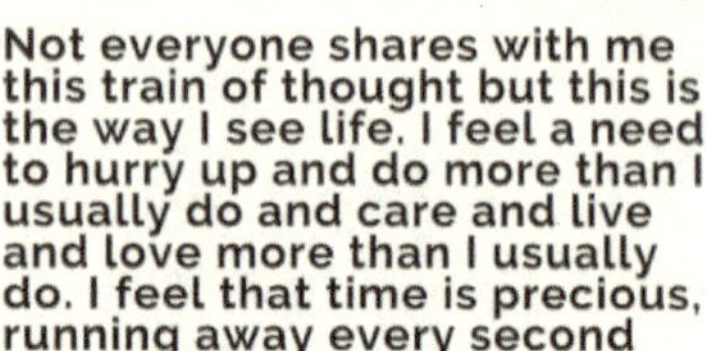

Not everyone shares with me this train of thought but this is the way I see life. I feel a need to hurry up and do more than I usually do and care and live and love more than I usually do. I feel that time is precious, running away every second and every minute of the day, and is therefore running out.

On a reflective note, I think that my life now is more valuable in terms of what I can contribute to society and to the people around me. I say this not because I get older and wiser every year. Contrary to this, I become more valuable each passing day not because of the natural flow of things: truth is, *there is less of me left today than when I was me yesterday*. Perhaps less in potential, in capacities, in inclination. That is where my increased value lies.

Not everyone shares with me this train of thought but this is the way I see life. I feel a need to hurry up and do more than I usually do and care and live and love more than I usually do. I feel that time is precious, running away every second and every minute of the day, and is therefore running out. Consequently, I must make haste, if I am to make good what Colin Coplin advised in his poem.

I became a Jack-of-many-trades. I was a face to many people, for a lot of events and activities. I could be compared to the playwright who initially hung around theaters, but was intent on learning the ropes, so he began setting up the stage and fitting the costumes. Then he went on to remembering, copying, memorizing, and delivering lines, and finally to directing and producing his own plays.

> I learned time management and working according to boundaries. I knew who I was and where my skills were best applied. Seemingly unconnected, the multiple roles that I took on in life, both welcome and unwelcome, allowed me to develop a combined skillset integral to my personal development and wellbeing, and to that of the people around me.

Taking on varied roles was not a deterrent to my personal growth. I learned time management and working according to boundaries. I knew who I was and where my skills were best applied. Psychology and understanding of the self were key to this. Seemingly unconnected, the multiple roles that I took on in life, both welcome and unwelcome, allowed me to develop a combined skillset integral to my personal development and wellbeing, and to that of the people around me.

Initially, when I was in high school, I did not know what I wanted to be when I grew up, though I cannot honestly say that any grownup had asked me that question. Nothing was clear to me. Nothing was determined. However, I realized that multiple roles gave me the space to explore different paths and presented me with different possibilities. I decided, "Well, I could choose from any one of them."

One could never imagine that my writing for the student publication and my part-time work as a writer for the Department of Health in Region IV would culminate in a book writer today! My being able to have solid knowledge of principles and theories of learning allowed for a certain degree of maneuverability on my part to readily adapt. The following event in my life testified to this.

As I mentioned earlier, I hoped to complete a four-year psychology degree in less time than required. I was in Manila for my freshman year. However, after completing just one semester, the family was dealt a cruel blow. My father became jobless! I had to return to the province immediately. He was a Scout Ranger for the Philippine military for sixteen years, before coming an Overseas Filipino Worker for the next couple of years. But his job turned out to be very difficult for him. His company in Saudi Arabia did not give its employees their wages on time. My father and his colleagues did not receive any compensation for several months, and the months stretched to almost two years. So my father had to come home, deciding to stay permanently.

I was working as a writer for the Department of Health at that time and had to travel twice a week to their main office in Project 4, Quezon City, to keep up with press release dates. The meager salary I received during this writing job somehow saw me through my studies in university until my father lost his job and decided to come home for good, and my brief stint so far at a university in Manila was exactly that – brief.

I ended up going back home, and tried my luck at finding jobs, but could not find one. Who would hire a high school graduate who had completed just one semester in university? I became, literally, a "school dropout" for a semester. Many people would not know about this until the publication of this book. I'm using this term very loosely in this narrative. I do not mean someone who intentionally dropped out of school and was never heard of afterwards but someone who, due to unforeseen circumstances, completed only a fraction of his studies.

And who would believe that this "school dropout" would go on to complete his studies, with honors, two doctorate degrees, one in psychology, and the other in management, only because he never gave up believing that he could make it? Who would know that the one who once sought scholarships is now providing scholarships for the college students in his hometown?

Carpe momentum. "Seize the moment" had always been one of my life truisms. It had guided me and I had followed it the best I could.

In retrospect, I was out of school for one more semester. The following year, I applied, and won, a four-year scholarship to study at the same university! My reaction to this was, first, astonishment! I could hardly believe that I won! My second reaction was a relief. Anyone associated with the university knew how tough the system was! And I was very blessed to have conquered it! The only requirement for this scholarship was that I should maintain my being a member of the student publication and obtain high grades according to the established university guidelines. This string of fortuitous events was the start of something big happening in my life.

This started it all. I got to choose my field of specialization and won a full scholarship that paid my way through university. I considered this a second chance given to me by my school. Other well-meaning students applied for the same scholarship but it was given to me. I won it. And one reason to celebrate my past would be this one. It gave me that much-needed push to truly think that I could do it – it was a boost to my confidence, to my self-worth! I promised to persevere, and to be consistent in the quality of my work.

Again, inspired by Colin Coplin, I finally found my place where the Good Things were and the impetus needed for all these to begin flowing into my life and be made manifest.

I was able to retain my part-time job in the Department of Department of Health's (DOH) headquarters, so I earned a little amount for my subsistence. I was grateful that I did not have to depend on my family for my allowance, seeing how things were even more difficult at home.

I would normally leave home on Thursdays to be on time for work there. Other student writers were there as well, writing for the Department that oversaw the health needs of an entire region. "Promotion of Health for the People" was its motto. The student writers were tasked with coming up with news features that showcased the health programs of the DOH in the region, like access to medicines, medical personnel, and facilities, and vaccination programs, all related to basic public health services, from the region down to the *barangay*, the smallest unit of government. Along the way, I became a leader among the student writers and gained their respect. *Carpe momentum.* "Seize the moment" had always been one of my life truisms. It had guided me and I had followed it the best I could.

> **After catching my mother sobbing silently in a corner of the house, I vowed to myself that I would never again allow my other siblings to experience the want and the need, the frustration, disappointment and humiliation that I endured. My mother, true to form, made enormous sacrifices and navigated life. She inspired me to do my best.**

My community engagements during this time in my life was superb because I gave my best to every task.

The real difficulty would lie in not having anything to eat if my allowances failed. I still remember those days when at four o'clock in the afternoon, my siblings and I had still not eaten our breakfast. Remember that my father for several months did not receive his wages abroad. When he came home, he became jobless and he remained so for many more months.

Nevertheless, because of my sheer strength of will and a very dogged determination, I was able to complete my tertiary education. Pride shone in the faces of my family! However, I very nearly missed my own graduation and the opportunity to receive the Batch Leadership Award! We did not have enough money for the fare to travel to my university! We searched all over the house for every little centavo we could find to have enough for transportation and only after finding some hidden coins did we sigh our collective sighs of relief! We found only just enough centavos to go! That very month, too, our electricity supply had been disconnected because of non-payment.

After catching my mother sobbing silently in a corner of the house, I vowed to myself that I would never again allow my other siblings to experience the want and the need, the frustration, disappointment and humiliation that I endured. My mother, true to form, made enormous sacrifices and navigated life almost entirely on her own as the primary breadwinner so that she could send all four of her children to school. She inspired me.

All things come through a mother after all. "Son," she would say, "your father isn't here. You're the man of the house now. Do the best you can for your siblings."

Happily, hearteningly, three days after graduation from university, I was already working in a Human Resource Department. Time slipped away so fast. Five years after that, I was already the director of that department.

This directorship in human resources opened another portal of interest for me. I felt that I was being called to a greater arena, a bigger venture. I could not stay any longer within the four walls of that department. I aimed to discover higher mountains to climb, greener pastures to see, and take on more significant challenges.

Minute day-to-day activities that comprised a series of actions and reactions, would appear with a speed that I could scarcely have imagined.

And all these, dear Reader, comprise the start of it all.

## Reflections

Key Insights: Draw from this Chapter your major takeaways.

1. ____________________________________________

____________________________________________

____________________________________________

2. ____________________________________________

____________________________________________

____________________________________________

3. ____________________________________________

____________________________________________

____________________________________________

Recount events in your life related to the Key Insights.

1. ____________________________________________

____________________________________________

____________________________________________

2. ____________________________________________

____________________________________________

____________________________________________

3. ____________________________________________

____________________________________________

____________________________________________

How can these Key Insights guide you and prepare you for life's present and future challenges?

1. ______________________________________________

______________________________________________

______________________________________________

2. ______________________________________________

______________________________________________

______________________________________________

3. ______________________________________________

______________________________________________

______________________________________________

Chapter 4

# Rising above the Waves

And He said
unto me,
My grace is
sufficient for thee:
for My strength is
made perfect
in weakness.

2 Corinthians 12:9

I grew up poor in the Philippines. My family had very little in terms of what would keep body and soul together. We lived with limited food and housing security, limited access to better health care, and increased likelihood of dropping out of school. However, ironic as it may seem, the maxim "failures create the pathways to successes" is true. On looking back, it becomes clear that troubles maketh the man.

For me, personally, three situations in my life brought the truth of this realization into sharp focus. Just as I learned from others, so, too can others learn from my experiences. The experiences of others help us not only to learn, but also to build, to create our own life.

**For me, personally, the situations in my life brought the truth of my realization into sharp focus. Just as I learned from others, so, too can others learn from my experiences. The experiences of others help us not only to learn, but also to build, to create our own life.**

The very first realization that I would say is that I decided not to remain poor. It started in my mind, where the battleground was, from a decision that I made. The fact is that people view the state of being poor as a hopeless quagmire, a sticky predicament that entraps and ensnares, and from which escape is impossible. Born poor, die poor. This was at least true to me until I reached forty-eight years of age, but I realized that this has become disputable beyond that age.

But what does it *really* mean to be poor in a country like the Philippines? I would like to show you, dear Reader, a glimpse of the field of economics, where a majority of its citizens are *not* created, nor treated, equal.

Statistics and poverty definitions vary, but according to the National Economic and Development Authority in the Philippines, the poor are individuals and families whose income falls below the poverty threshold or those who "cannot afford in a sustained manner to provide their minimum basic needs of food, health, education, housing, and other essential amenities of life."

According to the Philippine Statistics Authority, being poor in the Philippines means living below the threshold of P10,481 or P69.87 per day for a family of five (that is, $1.9 per person per day international poverty line in purchasing power). This resulted in tens of millions of Filipinos not meeting minimum standards of well-being. This figure has been contested by a number of sectors, claiming that this figure is "not an intelligent computation", and that a good place to start on a decent living wage is P42,000 a month for a family of five, according to Socioeconomic Planning Secretary Ernesto M. Pernia.

"The principal measure for poverty should be the cost of decent living. The minimum wage for eight hours of work should be equal to the cost of living," stated Leody de Guzman, the chair of the militant Bukluran ng Manggagawang Pilipino (BMP). Nobel Laureate in economics Joseph E. Stiglitz highlighted the need to examine other factors affecting well-being beyond income (Beyond GDP December 3, 2018). "If we want to put people first, we have to know what matters to them, what improves their well-being, and how we can supply more of whatever that is," he said (Beyond the data: What does being poor in the PHL mean? *Business Mirror*, April 18, 2019).

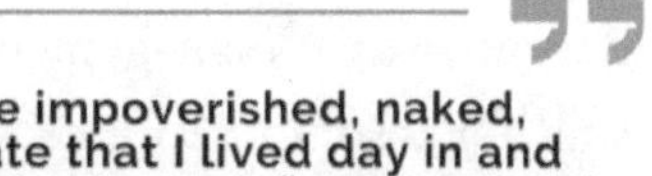

**The impoverished, naked, state that I lived day in and day out, was a "management case" that required thought and skill for resolution. Once I recognized it for what it was, it became a motivation, a driving force that made me think that I could overcome it, thus changing me into a better human being in the process and in the choices that I had to make in life.**

My family very obviously earned less than P42,000 a month, and this was an even much lower figure some twenty years ago. However, it did not truly matter to me what the poverty threshold was, whether it was P42,000 or even P10,481. I argued against accepting poverty as a natural occurrence in life. I stated my case for staring it down until it is forced to look away, to raging against the very existence of poverty and poverty thresholds! I strongly condemned succumbing to poverty, acquiescing to fate, thinking that it was much too much to overpower it! It probably was – but it was a fight that I intended to win!

I did not see eye-to-eye with the vast majority of poor people in my country. Truth to tell, I could not afford to view poverty the way they did, pardon the pun. My only option was to swim against the tide and not follow the crowd. This way of thinking about the world could be attributed to my genes or the way I was brought up (the so-called nature-nurture dilemma), I can not be sure. Nevertheless, that very poverty, for many, many years growing up, was, in fact, a challenge, a formidable one. If it had been absent from my life, in all likelihood I might not have turned out the way I did.

The impoverished, naked, state that I lived day in and day out, was a "management case" that required thought and skill for resolution. Once I recognized it for what it was, it became a motivation, a driving force that made me think that I could overcome it, thus changing me into a better human being in the process and in the choices that I had to make in life. Today, I believe that I exceeded all expectations. Social, economic, psychological. I needed to do more to survive, so I became more in that process of survival.

There is an important lesson to learn here. I believe that surviving is good, but *thriving* resembles more the reality of being in the world and contributing something to the world. I developed a survival system that let me beat all the odds. Sherwood's Survivor's Club (2009) lists twelve survival traits that I used to draw strength from. These are adaptability, resilience, faith, hope, purpose, tenacity, love, empathy, intelligence, ingenuity, flow, and instinct.

Furthermore, according to Kauffman (2016), with variations from Kramler (2004), four factors determine who survives and thrives. The first is a will to survive. Having the right attitude is key. This involves accepting one's reality while believing that things will eventually change. It is about having a purpose. The second is the ability of the survivor to break down tasks into smaller tasks, no matter how small, that could be completed. Taking baby steps helps the survivor to not be overwhelmed by the enormity of their situation. The third is applied knowledge. Knowledge is necessary, but being able to use it and apply it in a survival situation is what is important to survive. The fourth is conditioning. The body should be healthy and engaged in some reasonable physical exercise. Healthy people have a better chance of surviving.

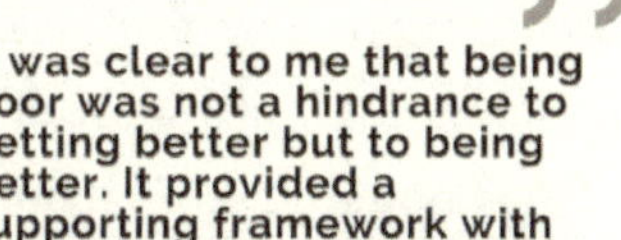

It was clear to me that being poor was not a hindrance to getting better but to being better. It provided a supporting framework with safe landings. Climbing the stairway led me towards the achievement of things hoped for by using extraordinary means. Climbing that stairway and jumping over a series of hurdles was special, something to benefit from.

Thus the first part of the threefold realization is that, right at the outset, it was clear to me that being poor was not a hindrance to getting better, to *being* better. Rather, it was a stairway. It provided a supporting framework with safe landings to move from one level, i.e. phase of my life to another. Climbing this stairway led me towards the achievement of things hoped for by using extraordinary means, which to others may be routine, but to me, climbing that stairway and jumping over a series of hurdles was special, something to benefit from.

Although it sometimes seemed as though I had too much on my plate, I tried to look at things positively, believing that all would be well in the end if I did not lose hope. I viewed the details happening in my life as a tapestry that must be woven, the minutiae contributing to a beautiful landscape.

Greatness, after all, is a series of small things done well, according to Eric Thomas, and I persisted in hope and faith, which is the "substance of things hoped for, the evidence of things not seen…" (Hebrews 11:1) believing that all will be well in the end.

The second realization falls under an unintentional man-made catastrophe, the effects of which would haunt me and my family for many years to come. I was about to graduate from college at age twenty when our ancestral home in Baras, Rizal, little and humble as it was, was engulfed by fire and completely destroyed. A relative, who chanced to be at home that time when everybody was out, did not take sensible precautionary measures in using the kitchen firewood and in lighting the fire for cooking his dinner.

> Although it sometimes seemed as though I had too much on my plate, I tried to look at things positively, believing that all would be well in the end if I did not lose hope. I viewed the details happening in my life as a tapestry that must be woven, the minutiae contributing to a beautiful landscape. Greatness, after all, is a series of small things done well.

Fortunately, my parents and siblings were not home when the calamity happened. I received a call informing me that the house was already gone. No one got hurt, yes, but the fire burned down everything that the family possessed in this world, including the tiny *sari-sari* store. It broke everyone's hearts and fear started to creep in while we sorted through the ashes and debris, trying to see if there was something – *anything* - that could still be salvaged. The fear was compounded by the certainty that we were experiencing more than the usual share of earthly troubles and that we would have to begin all over again, literally and figuratively.

Dear reader, I've already told you that my father could not financially support the family after coming back home from being an Overseas Filipino Worker. He experienced major delays in receiving wages. For almost two years, he did not receive anything. So after the fire, there we were. Gaunt and hungry, haggard, sleepless, homeless. Sympathetic relatives took us in, not all in one house of course - we were dispersed among kind folks.

This was one of the most tumultuous and discouraging times in our lives. It would have been very easy for us to give up – on each other, on life. However, we decided to be strong. We needed to be strong. Being the eldest, I decided that no one would give up. A consensus was reached that we would not let this latest drawback drag us down. If we were to survive, we needed to do something fast to be able to eke out a living.

It was decided that, temporarily at least, the family would sell snacks, or *yema*, a milky-creamy, custard confectionary, Filipino dessert made of caramelized milk, besides the regular firewood and charcoal that we had already been selling and which were earning for the family a small, steady income.

The *yema* ingredients were readily available. On top of canned goods and noodles, there would be condensed milk distributed by the health center for the town's poor people. We would use this condensed milk. We would borrow a kilo of brown sugar, a carton of white eggs, and some *mantequilla* (margarine) from Aling Magnaye, whose store was a stone's throw away from home, to be paid back after we would have made some sales (I was sure she would understand our plight!). We would add coconut strips, or even peanuts, to make them more saleable. There were plenty of young coconuts from the nearby coconut grove. The peanuts were also from Aling Magnaye's store. We would be cooking on an open fire and firewood would not be a problem, either.

We put the *yema* in little organic boxes made from banana leaves then sold them house-to-house rather than selling them out front in our small store. People bought them since they found our *yema* delicious and because they knew that we needed the money.

After all the *yema* boxes, firewood, and charcoal had been sold, we would visit Aling Magnaye to pay her what we owed for the day, then buy from her a few kilos of rice, sardines (one tin can green, the other, red, to even out the spicy taste), and at worst, some salt we spread on rice uncooked, stirred egg just to have a meal. We would go back to wherever we were staying temporarily, cook what we bought, then have our first meal of the day, at 3:00 or 4:00 in the afternoon.

We asked what we could do, being in the very center of what was a dire situation. Wasn't there a way for us to escape this difficult life? Had the Lord any reason for why our family should need to undergo these painful and humiliating trials? Would He have any specific plans for us?

The third realization that I wanted to share with you was to make do with whatever you have, and, if needs be, create something new from the ground up. It does not have to be grand or lavish, as long as your most pressing need is met.

The day when I would graduate from university was drawing near. The family was excited because, being the eldest, I would be the first to complete tertiary education. However, I still did not have anything decent to wear. We did not have enough money to buy an off-the-rack polo shirt and trousers and shoes from a department store, where most clients would go for clothes for special occasions. My grandmother, resourceful as she was, was a pillar of strength for me and my siblings. She decided that since she knew basic sewing and clothes measurements, she would hand-sew my graduation apparel. Everyone wondered how it would turn out.

After taking my measurements (collar, chest, sleeve, waist, hips, inside leg, outside leg), she set out to buy some durable fabric from the *talipapa* or marketplace, where cloths and textiles were sold by the yards on the street. Initially torn between a short-sleeved polo or a long-sleeved one, she finally decided on the latter since she was able to buy just enough material. She sat down to work on the long-sleeved polo first, then making a pair of loose pants to go with it. After all the sewing and darning was done, I tried them on to see the fit and found that they were very well made. I was very pleased and thanked her profusely. For shoes, well, my old pair of synthetic leather ones sufficed.

When graduation day came, however, much to our chagrin, we found out that not a single centavo was to be found anywhere. We were trying to collect enough coins for our transportation fare. We would be riding the jeepney, a minibus-like public utility vehicles, serving as the most popular means of public transportation in the Philippines, across town to the next town where the university was situated.

> My path led uphill, the climb torturous and bumpy, but I soldiered on. I knew that this uphill climb would position me for a better view of what I could accomplish in life. This uphill climb also ensured that I gave idleness and unproductivity a wide berth. It introduced me to Perseverance, my bosom friend and constant companion, without which I would not be where I am now.

Thankfully, a relative very kindly lent us a few pesos, enough for the fare.

I was able to march proudly up to the graduation stage once my name was called. I received the Leadership Excellence Award to the delight of my family who, like me, almost did not make it to the graduation hall.

A favorite cousin, Francis, traveled from the capital city Manila to attend my graduation, telling the family that my father had told him months ago that my graduation would be on that date. He was asked by my father to be with me in his stead.

Excitement, encouragement and hope were palpable in the air. Hopeful indeed we were because, finally, the college diploma would lead me to a well-paid job that would equal a good roof above our heads and square meals on the table. It was hoped that the family could relax a bit in the selling of charcoal, firewood, and *yema*, that we could eat substantial meals each day and not skip any, buy the things that we needed, and go to places we needed to go without having someone loan us the transportation fare.

My path led uphill, the climb torturous and bumpy, but I soldiered on. I knew that this uphill climb would position me for a better vie w of what I could accomplish in life. This uphill climb also ensured that I gave idleness and unproductivity a wide berth. It introduced me to Perseverance, my bosom friend and constant companion, without which I would not be where I am now.

For me, attitude spelled the difference. Even if we can't always control what life throws at us, we can control our attitude.

I realized that the more I saw myself as hopeless, the more I would learn about hopelessness. The more I felt victimized by the series of unfortunate events which started when I was but a young lad, the more helpless I felt, and the more I blamed everyone around me. The more I attributed bad luck to my parents, siblings, and relatives, the more guilty I felt because I knew that they were in exactly in the same boat as I was, also suffering.

It was a vicious cycle, a never-ending merry-go-round that offered no escape. So I decided to change my attitude, my frame of reference. Something needed to change. I was sick and tired of being sick and tired!

You see, dear Reader, the battle always starts in the mind. If there is no enemy within, the enemy outside can do us no harm (African proverb). The best way to win this battle that rages from within is by practicing the kind of thinking outlined in Philippians 4:8. "Finally, brothers and sisters, whatever is true, whatever is noble, whatever is right, whatever is pure, whatever is lovely, whatever is admirable – if anything is excellent and praiseworthy – *think* about these things."

However, things would continue to challenge our resolve.

After the ceremony, on coming back home, we came upon a dark house. The electricity had been cut because of unpaid bills. After lighting a few gas lamps, and kindling some firewood, we could not celebrate because there was no food. Everyone was intensely disappointed, especially Mother. My cousin who was with us during the graduation ceremony informed us that he would need to go back to Manila. Mother offered him her profuse apologies because of the state of the darkened house and the absence of graduation refreshments. Later, I caught her weeping silently and I hugged her, promising that things would be alright. I have already received my college degree and would soon be able to find work, I consoled her. Mother solemnly gave her promise to us that one day, the whole family would feast on sumptuous foods, that we would have a decent home, that we would wear decent clothes, and all my other siblings would finish their studies.

So, there was I, dear Reader. I present to you again these three generalizations. One, the desire to escape poverty took root in my mind. Two, a conflagration could not quench my dreams. Three, something new could be created if the need and the will were huge enough.

These three truths are yours for the taking. Do what you will with them. You may accept them and allow them to accompany you on your journey in life. Or you may negate them and point out all their flaws. No matter. What was lived was lived. I am not here to persuade you to think this or that, to decide on doing this or that. I aim to simply narrate to you the truths in my life, to affirm the events as they happened, without warning, and how each hammer-and-tongs event bewildered and confused me. I groped for a steady rock to hang on to. Finally, I gained enough strength to accept that each of the trials and difficulties in my life had been sent to me for a definite purpose. That purpose was not to put me down but to strengthen me.

The days stretched on, becoming weeks, months, years. After the fire, we were able to slowly rebuild what was lost from the ground up. Unhappily, my sister Tina also experienced what happened to me (electricity was also cut on her graduation day!). But never again! So my two other brothers, Raymond and Jonas, whom I sent to school and provided all their academic needs for, graduated with electricity in the house because the electric bills had been paid for and on time!

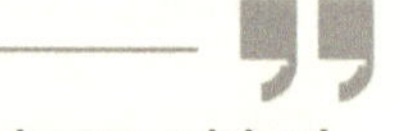

> I grew up in an impoverished community wherein people still took the time to be kind to one another, and to help one another out. I was very easily moved when I saw people suffer. I felt their pain, their trauma, as if they were my own. I lived what Nicholas Sparks said. Without suffering, there'd be no compassion.

Eventually, my family and I were able to rise slowly from the ashes. Tina eventually married a US Navy man and created a loving family and built her own home. Ultimately, after years of grueling hard work as a call center agent, as a consultant at a private hospital, and as a university instructor (juggling all these activities at the same time), I was also able to buy properties for myself and purchase a brand-new car. I sent Raymond and Jonas to school, too, and gave them hope to thrive.

The entire family needed all the courage, strength, and determination in the world to be able to produce something from scratch, literally and figuratively. However, we could not have risen entirely on our own accord. Although I grew up in an impoverished community, people still took the time to be kind to one another, and to help one another out. This was the reason why kindness and compassion were ingrained in me. They were second nature, my second skin. I was very easily moved when I saw people suffer. I felt their pain, their trauma, as if they were my own. I lived what Nicholas Sparks said. Without suffering, there'd be no compassion.

By the sweat of my brow, by determination and mental acuity, and with the love and support of God's instruments, the people around me, I continued my post-graduate studies after graduating from college. While working full time, I obtained a master's degree in Organizational Psychology, a PhD in Counselling Psychology, a post-doctoral bridge to Business Management, and a second PhD in Human Resource Management. I know that these are academic laurels, but, at the same time, these are God's marvelous opportunities, too, as I can serve the community with integrity. After earning these degrees, my range of influence would now encompass greater heights.

The three important failures and realizations that I narrated in this chapter made me a better human being, I believe, if not the best version of myself. I did not let the heartaches and the hardships of the past overshadow me. Truly, it was a very steep climb upward but grit, purposefulness, forbearance, and a stout heart brought their sure rewards.

## Reflections

Key Insights: Draw from this Chapter your major takeaways.

1. ______________________________

______________________________

______________________________

2. ______________________________

______________________________

______________________________

3. ______________________________

______________________________

______________________________

Recount events in your life related to the Key Insights.

1. ______________________________

______________________________

______________________________

2. ______________________________

______________________________

______________________________

3. ______________________________

______________________________

______________________________

How can these Key Insights guide you and prepare you for life's present and future challenges?

1. ______________________________________________

______________________________________________

______________________________________________

2. ______________________________________________

______________________________________________

______________________________________________

3. ______________________________________________

______________________________________________

______________________________________________

## Chapter 5

# Measure of Service to Humanity

No one is useless in this world who lightens the burdens of another.

CHARLES DICKENS

How do we all create a world the way it should be created? How can the future be reinvented? Is it even remotely possible to reorganize our social and economic foundations, to create new designs of life and living, after the COVID-19 pandemic?

> Prioritizing people, and placing them squarely back on the stratagems used in dealing with the world, will solve many of our major dilemmas and upheavals.

According to Paulo Coelho (2000), "When we least expect it, life sets us a challenge to test our courage and willingness to change; at such a moment, there is no point in pretending that nothing has happened or in saying that we are not ready. The challenge will not wait. Life does not look back. A week is more than enough time for us to decide whether or not to accept our destiny."

We need a fundamental reform that puts people back at the heart of economic and social systems and does not relegate them to the sidelines.

In this chapter, I would like to highlight this paramount need of putting people back at the heart of the things that we do, going back to the original goal, which is to educate the heart more than the mind, feed the heart with positivity, hope, and action to create the world that we need. This is the least we could do if we want to leave lasting value to the next generation. I believe that prioritizing people, and placing them squarely back on the stratagems used in dealing with the world, will solve many of our major dilemmas and upheavals.

I put forward my personal philosophy in this regard, that the measure of our service to humanity is equal to the amount of love we pour into our selfless acts. This is the sum total of the range of experiences that I want to share in this chapter.

In Baras, my birthplace, the smallest town in Rizal province, if one were to use a gauge to measure the happiness of its citizens, he would simply ask one quintessential question: How far has the family made steps to ensure that the children study - and stay - in school? The family unit revolves around understanding the importance children being educated and being able to complete their education. What actions have been taken? Has the father gotten himself a job as a truck driver in Saudi Arabia? Or has the mother sent her application to Singapore as a domestic worker? Has the carabao been sold? Has the property been leased? Has that pair of earrings, or that necklace, or that watch, been pawned? It was always, "Get an education", "Finish college", "Get a degree." Education was the most valuable legacy that parents could bequeath their children since no one could steal knowledge and wisdom away from them.

That was the daily mantra for children of all ages. "Mag-aral kang mabuti" (Study well). As soon as a child said goodbye to his parents in the morning with the usual kissing of hands, saying, "Papasok na po ako" (I'm leaving now for school), the formal and predictable "Mag-aral kang mabuti" would always follow. This was an almost sacred exchange that was essentially the guiding philosophy of the family. I believe that this way of thinking also applies to the majority of families in the Philippines, not only in Baras.

I have always viewed education as a means to achieving one's end, not only in providing for self and family but also for more noble reasons. What better way to have the greatest possible impact on people by teaching them what I know? Engaging in the multifaceted ways of educating diverse individuals is a stairway to helping them achieve their aims in life, their aspirations, their ambitions. Education should be free and no one should be deprived of any learning opportunity.

Education teaches one to be part of humanity. It teaches compassion, sympathy, generosity, and respect. It appeals to someone's sense of kind-heartedness, understanding, and goodwill. It is a role that must be taken up if one were to contribute to the community and to society.

Education should be tied up with the selfless giving of time and expertise. I did just that when, in the early part of my career, I became a member of a church choir that was not only concerned with singing during worship but also more importantly, concerned with the plight of the needy.

The Young Mission Apostle Choir (YMAC) of Baras, Rizal, was not just a church choir but also a group that cared for the destitute - the lost, the least, the last. I was the second president in this group's history. Comprised of about twenty members and wearing our bright green t-shirts, we would sing carols during the Christmas season trying to raise both funds for and awareness of the poor in the community. We sang for peace on earth, laughter all around, serenity, reflective lives, and hearts open in reaching out to the poor without any hope of reward. We bought and distributed for free among the needy some of the most basic things – rice, canned goods, slippers. What was most important, however, was our spiritual and emotional engagements with them – love, foremost – without which our faith would simply be empty "resounding gongs and clanging cymbals" (I Corinthians 13:1).

However, educating the heart, more than the mind, is what is essential. In so doing, we become more humane and more able to love individuals who are not even related to us, whom we have not even met. This is something that strongly resonates with me, as feeding the mind with positivity topples what is called the learned helplessness response, or, in psychology, the "mental state in which an organism is forced to bear aversive stimuli, or stimuli that are painful or otherwise unpleasant, and becomes unable or unwilling to avoid subsequent encounters with those stimuli, even if they are 'escapable', presumably because it has learned that it cannot control the situation" (Nolen, 2009).

I take learned helplessness to mean the attitude of accepting what fate offers and not making the necessary conscious and rational move to go against it. Everything relates to having the right mindset. This is precisely the reason why I say educating the heart is more essential than educating the mind. The mind sometimes gets fixed on something and does not accept change easily. A fixed mindset does not always help the individual that possesses it. His mind tortures him and becomes a burden to him even if he has the power to escape its negativity and helplessness.

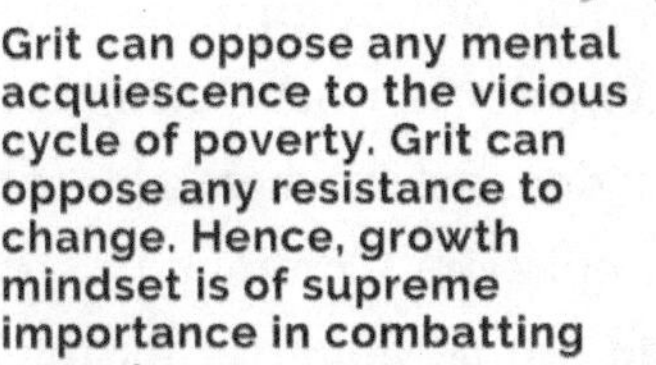


Angela Duckworth's *Grit: The Power of Passion and Perseverance* (2016) has influenced my thinking in this area. She made 'grit' the leading buzzword in education-policy circles. According to her, grit is passion and perseverance for long-term goals and is not related to IQ but to conscientiousness and character education. On this premise, Duckworth is working towards the expansion of school instruction beyond solely cognitive factors.

My point here is that grit can oppose any mental acquiescence to the vicious cycle of poverty. Grit can oppose any resistance to change. Again, the growth mindset is of supreme importance in combatting poverty.

> **Community service is, after all, unpaid work, and people volunteer for the betterment of the community. Structures and resources are used to address specific needs that eventually foster emancipation, goodwill, and empowerment of community members.**

We should therefore take good care of both heart and mind if care for the heart cannot take precedence.

Again, the measure of one's service to humanity equals the amount of love that fills those selfless acts. This service to humanity is what's being learned in both community and religious work, where a lot of things are always, always, await completion. Community service is, after all, unpaid work, and people volunteer for the betterment of the community. Structures and resources are used to address specific needs that eventually foster emancipation, goodwill, and empowerment of community members.

The presence of a gracious, giving heart lays the foundation, *is* the foundation. It is akin to building a tower by layering bricks one by one. Each brick is a good deed, a selfless act, that we put on top of another to create a mural, a meaning, a connection, an understanding.

We toil. We labor. We add love to these bricks that we put up, one after the other. We put each one up, bit by bit, until the bricks reach the point where we want them to go, and then when we look up, we become amazed that the tower has grown really high, really grand, and really picturesque. The tower is now the product of our meticulous, painstaking, minute labor. It has become the product of our selfless acts of love.

> **A faucet can only be made useful when it is attached to a pipe or a reservoir. The faucet controls the flow of water out of the pipe. Education is the reservoir of knowledge. The faucet is our ability to control what flows through the pipe. This ability is made strong or weak based on our preparedness, the timing, the reception, and, sometimes, the support of those around us.**

One Christmas, the church decided that YMAC would put up a

benefit show, an evening of the seasonal music and carols. We distributed tickets at a fair price. It was decided that the proceeds would go to the various communities the church was serving, especially to the impoverished people living on the outskirts. The tickets were sold out! The concert was a success! We were able to distribute food, clothing, and Christmas toys to the needy! Part of the proceeds created meaningful projects for the community's recycling programs and also provided for the upkeep of the church's musical instruments.

One can always do more besides donating money. Time and expertise are both needed in small and big communities. I believe that to be able to touch other people's hearts and minds, selfless acts of love and devotion must be very clear even at the outset of planning and developing programs. Yes, plans and programs are indeed essential in establishing communities and community rapport – but it takes more than plans and programs to make people believe the words that we are saying. They see our intentions and purposes, more than our pious preaching.

I equate this to a faucet that can only be made useful when it is attached to a pipe or a reservoir. The faucet controls the flow of water out of the pipe. Education is the reservoir of knowledge. The faucet is our ability to control what flows through the pipe. This ability is made strong or weak based on our preparedness, the timing, the reception, and, sometimes, the support of those around us.

Time passed. I decided to pursue a master's degree. An MA would qualify me to teach at university. I was a human resource manager at that time and, on reflection, I knew that I would not be employed in an HR department for the rest of my life. A vision came to me. I knew what I should become and what I should do to realize that vision. I needed to pursue a higher degree to equip myself with the technical ability to engage students enrolled in tertiary education.

Always a firm believer in educating the heart even more than the mind, I continued with my community engagement in the church. I was also teaching part-time at De La Salle University - Dasmariñas, having started in 2000, and completed was able to complete my master's degree in Organizational Psychology in 2002. My goal was to teach full-time at this University now that I was a master's degree holder.

One other very important community organization I became involved with was the Boy Scouts of the Philippines, Manila Chapter. The BSP director, Efren, happened to be a good friend of mine. He encouraged me to train leaders, who turned out to be key school officials and principals in schools in Manila, in addition to teachers. I was a Boy Scout in my younger years in Baras. Remember that episode of the eraser-throwing teacher? I said that I wiped the chalk dust off my face with my Boy Scout handkerchief. But that was the only Boy Scout experience that I could relate to. Training principals and school heads on the merits and rigors of scouting was a completely different ball game. "On my honor, I will do my best to do my duty for God and my country and to obey the Scout Law, to help other people at all times, to keep myself physically strong, mentally awake, and morally straight." This was a very solemn oath that was not to be taken lightly.

Training people so that they, too, could train others, began to occupy my mind. What could be done so that a majority could benefit? This goes beyond mere utilitarianism. It was a passion, a driving force to keep the light burning even on the darkest of days that ultimately led me to the kind of community engagement that I began to increasingly immerse myself in.

I needed to develop myself professionally to become more credible, to be the kind of influencer that people would like to listen to. That community work in De La Salle University-Dasmariñas provided me with opportunities to eventually reach out to male municipal inmates located in the town (now a city). I developed a program specifically for these men which included basic adult literacy classes, art therapy classes, and counseling sessions. These inmates eventually became respondents when I embarked on my doctoral dissertation.

> **Hope is crucial. Take hope away and the person dies. Only a series of selfless acts of love, compassion, devotion, and humanity could rescue a hopeless person from the abyss.**

Further on, the kind of community work that I had been doing had been reflective of the kind of outcome I have had in my educational endeavor. I provided counseling to male jail inmates, which enabled me to really see them, to see through the barriers they had erected their pain and anguish, to see their guilt and shame and regret, to look beyond the mere physical and into their souls. This is something not typically observed by a typical *tao*, a typical person. The art therapy that I managed with the inmates provides insights into the nature of their true selves. I would tell them that hope is a good thing because it never dies, and that they should be relentless in their pursuit of both hope and well-being, despite their very real predicaments.

Hope is crucial. Take hope away and the person dies. Only a series of selfless acts of love, compassion, devotion, and humanity could rescue a hopeless person from the abyss.

## Reflections

Key Insights: Draw from this Chapter your major takeaways.

1. ______________________________

______________________________

______________________________

2. ______________________________

______________________________

______________________________

3. ______________________________

______________________________

______________________________

Recount events in your life related to the Key Insights.

1. ______________________________

______________________________

______________________________

2. ______________________________

______________________________

______________________________

3. ______________________________

______________________________

______________________________

How can these Key Insights guide you and prepare you for life's present and future challenges?

1. ______________________________________________

______________________________________________

______________________________________________

2. ______________________________________________

______________________________________________

______________________________________________

3. ______________________________________________

______________________________________________

______________________________________________

Chapter 6

# The Heart of Community Service

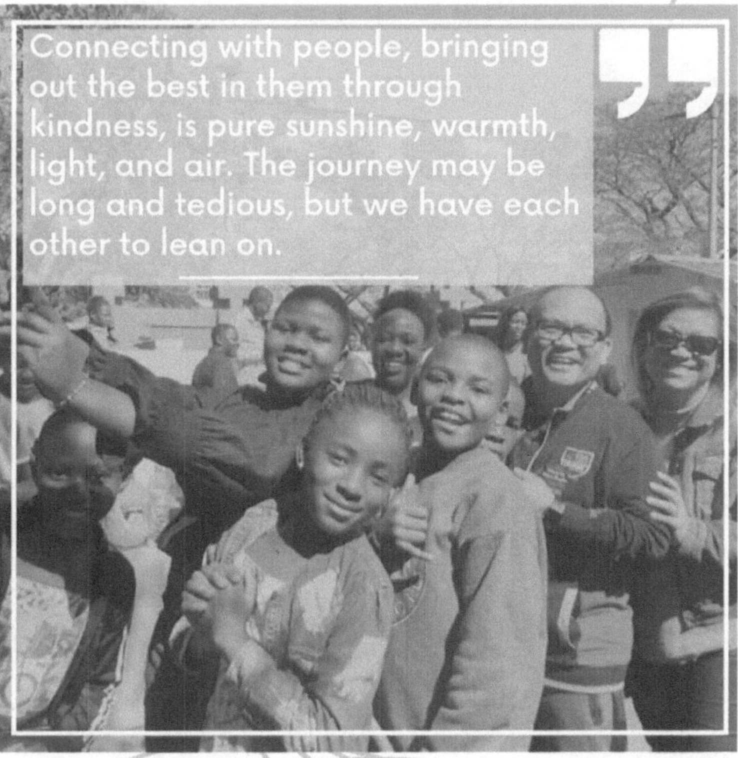

> Unexpected kindness is the most powerful, least costly, and most underrated agent of human change.
>
> Bob Kerrey

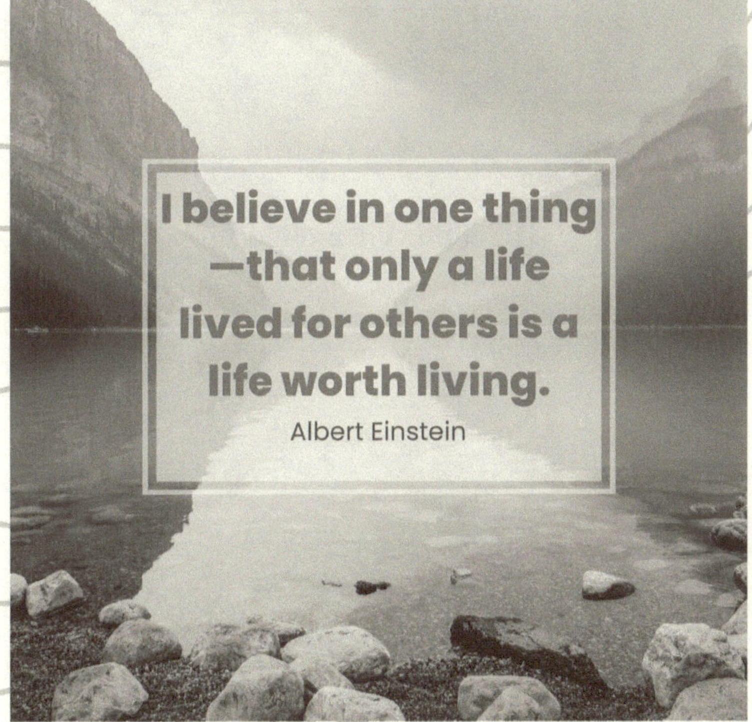
I believe in one thing
—that only a life
lived for others is a
life worth living.
Albert Einstein

Nobody cares how much you know,
until they know how much you care.
THEODORE ROOSEVELT

Leprosy, or Hansen's disease, is a chronic infectious disease caused by a mycobacterium (*Mycobacterium leprae*) affecting especially the skin and peripheral nerves and characterized by the formation of nodules or macules that enlarge and spread accompanied by loss of sensation with eventual paralysis, wasting of muscle, and production of deformities (Merriam-Webster Online Dictionary).

Imagine this scenario, dear Reader. On an educational field trip during high school, the school took the students, not to a zoo, a cultural center, or a home for the aged. The place that we visited was a leprosy mission center. A lot of bother and bustle happened in getting parental permission since, during that time, leprosy was known to be a highly communicable disease! (I did not know what the school administration was thinking, exposing students and faculty to a dreaded disease that way!) Today, we know that it isn't that contagious really. People can catch it only if they come into close and repeated contact with someone with untreated leprosy. Anyway, parental permission was granted but not without trepidation and worry.

It took the bus ferrying the students and a few teachers almost three hours to reach the leprosy mission center. After all the necessary protocol and introductions had been made, the director of the center began the tour of the facility. The students observed the patients at this leprosy mission house from a "safe distance" and were able to see, while the director was explaining, such conditions as severe skin sores causing disfigurements, lumps and bumps, and nerve damage in the arms and legs. Someone was missing a nose; another, all digits in his left hand; still another, both his ears. I could not help but stare at a man who had a missing right leg while the director was informing the huddled assembly that leprosy had been around since ancient times and outbreaks have affected people on every continent.

Witnessing firsthand the pain, suffering, and embarrassment endured by the lepers stunned me at the very core of my being. In my mind, I questioned the wisdom, rightness, and ethics of the mission center, and of my own school, in allowing outsiders to observe these patients, akin to how animals are presented and observed in cages in a zoo. In the center's mini-hospital, the students gawked and stared in stupid silence while the patients tried their best to hide their deformities by lying in fetal position - the backs were curved, heads were bowed, and limbs were bent and drawn up to the torso. I cried silently, seeing how my fellow human beings were being treated nonchalantly and without any care, with total disregard for their feelings, exposing their vulnerability to visitors who did not know the first thing about the disease and how we could very easily be infected as well.

Dear Reader, I'm narrating this part of my life because the pain and suffering that I witnessed that day at the leprosy mission center impressed in my heart and mind an even higher level of compassion for my fellowmen. It was humanity that cried out from the deepest recesses of my being, how one man's callous behavior could spell the difference between trauma and survival.

Compassion is the sympathetic consciousness of others' distress together with a desire to alleviate it (Merriam-Webster Online Dictionary). I would like to highlight the idea that everyone can be extraordinary, or exceptional or even remarkably noteworthy. However, a basic ingredient must be present for that to happen to an individual, an internalization and a practice of unusual compassion and kindness. This is uncommon virtue. This is kindness taken to another level, at a much higher plane.

The story of the Good Samaritan illustrates a perfect example. The Samaritan did not think about race or religion or status when he decided to stop and examine the condition of the dying man. This thousand-year-old parable has lessons to teach the modern world. A willingness to help is useless unless it is accompanied by actions. But in the internet-crazed world, photos of the half-dead man would probably end up on social media way before the man could even be taken to hospital. We probably would feel bad about what happened to the man but very few would probably dare do something to help. Would we be the priest and the Levite who walked away? Or the Samaritan who stayed to help?

I believe that we all have the power and the ability to be kind and compassionate. These are God-given characteristics since we have been created in His image. However, this power does not end there. This is the power that has serious, earnest potential, that is waiting to be let loose into where we could create the most positive results and ramifications. And to me, that environment where I was able to let loose the power of kindness and compassion and where I was able to give the greatest positive effects was communities, which have always held a special place in my heart.

In my witnessing the suffering of the lepers, a small prayer of gratitude to the Lord did cross my mind because I was not in the same situation. I was free from any malady of body and mind, capable to engage and excel in diverse activities. But appalling suffering and torment put one within the bounds of the realities of life and shake us into the cognizance of human frailties. They keep us grounded and sensible. This is the exact place where kindness and compassion could take deep and proper roots.

People can exhibit cognitive dissonance at times. This is the state of having inconsistent thoughts, beliefs, or attitudes, especially as relating to behavioral decisions and attitude change (Oxford Languages). A certain disconnect exists, an incongruence between what we think and feel and what we exhibit. It describes a mental discomfort that results from holding two conflicting sets of values and beliefs (when people smoke even if they know that smoking causes cancer, or to love someone who is difficult to love).

Social experiments have proven that once we think that we are being observed, we tend to show one kind of behavior, or the lack of it, even if we are thinking of something different to do. Disassociation and seclusion happen here at times but these should not be the case. When we help an old man cross the street, we do so because we know that he's frail and moves slowly, traits that could put his life in jeopardy when crossing the street. We don't look at him as someone who's a burden to society and must be gotten rid of one way or the other. And so, without prior experiences with trauma, pain, suffering, vulnerability, dissolution, and segregation, one would not feel any of these sensibilities and therefore would not, and could not, exhibit genuine, heartfelt kindness and compassion toward others.

I, therefore, say that the heart of community service, real community service, would be genuine feelings, sensitivities, an inclination toward the suffering of others, and a strong inherent proclivity to help and support. This propensity to assist will result in actual, concrete, and factual deeds of kindness and compassion, essentially similar to what the Good Samaritan did.

Random acts of kindness and compassion are simply that, random. They unintentionally and arbitrarily come into our lives as if to test us, how far we could go, we would go. Will we be bystanders and onlookers? Hyping over social media and the news the tragedy that was unfolding before our very eyes? Or do we choose to take action and be part of the scene actively? Any happenstance that may need our involvement can serve as mileposts or turning points when our lives could change dramatically, or even extraordinarily, but always for the better because the positive traits of kindness and compassion have been part and parcel of the event.

An experience that I had concerning random acts of kindness concerned a student that I thought I would say hello to. It was the beginning of the semester and I noticed a girl standing alone near the terrace of the fourth floor level of the building where I taught. I did not know the girl who would turn out to be my student in my afternoon class. I smiled and said hi to her. She looked at me and smiled back. We got into small talk and I wished her well before walking away to my class.

That afternoon, I met the same girl inside the classroom. She presented her registration form. Indeed, she would be my student. I learned later that day that when I saw her on the terrace, she was contemplating ending her life by jumping. A random act of greeting and a hello from a stranger changed her mind and saved her life. She thought, If this guy was bothered enough to notice her, go forward to her, smile at her, say hello to her, show her a little cognition and kindness, then, possibly, there would be a chance that life could be a little kinder to her, too.

And so it came to pass. The girl turned out to be one of my most brilliant students, and one of those most involved with leadership and community work among her peers. Her own life and thoughts of self-harm, how she was able to be drawn away from it by a very simple act of random kindness and compassion from a stranger, were the turning point and basis of her narrative.

In other words, had I not given my attention and a fraction of my time to this one poor soul who turned out to be completely alone, unhappy, and in dire need of companionship, both our stories could have ended very differently.

Connecting with people, bringing out the best in them through kindness and compassion, random the experience may be, is pure sunshine and warmth, light and air. Shadows disappear and spots and clouds vanish. We can hold hands and move forward with our lives. The journey may be long and tedious, but we have each other to lean on.

## Reflections

Key Insights: Draw from this Chapter your major takeaways.

1. ____________________________________________

____________________________________________

____________________________________________

2. ____________________________________________

____________________________________________

____________________________________________

3. ____________________________________________

____________________________________________

____________________________________________

Recount events in your life related to the Key Insights.

1. ____________________________________________

____________________________________________

____________________________________________

2. ____________________________________________

____________________________________________

____________________________________________

3. ____________________________________________

____________________________________________

____________________________________________

How can these Key Insights guide you and prepare you for life's present and future challenges?

1. ____________________________________________

____________________________________________

____________________________________________

2. ____________________________________________

____________________________________________

____________________________________________

3. ____________________________________________

____________________________________________

____________________________________________

## Chapter 7

# The Bad in Good, the Good in Bad

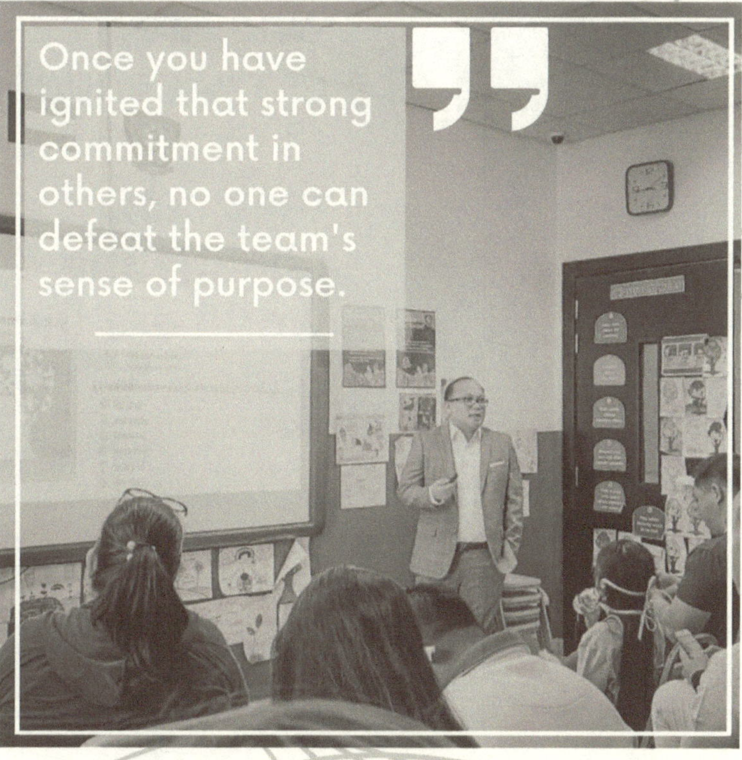

> The ones who are crazy enough to think that they can change the world are the ones who do.
>
> STEVE JOBS

One day, Pooh decided to invite all the animals in the forest to celebrate his birthday. He made all trimmings and decorations and prepared all the sumptuous foods himself, including a huge honey cake. He sent out party invitations to everybody, knowing that the animals would come to celebrate with him. The big day came! The invitation said 3 o'clock but at 4 o'clock, only a handful of animals had shown themselves. 5 o'clock came, then 6 o'clock. Still only a few were present. Pooh felt very bad, thinking that if the animals liked him, they would have come. Owl said, "It's not you. It's them. You had a delicious honey cake but some of them weren't ready to taste it!"

Dear Reader, the very same scenario happened to me, sadly, quite a number of times in the past. I would be involved in setting up very important events where numerous community leaders were expected to come and lend a hand. The team would send out missives and invitations, explaining the purpose of the event and the urgency of it happening. Then disappointment would dawn because only a few of those who got invited to the events would physically turn up.

Many different kinds of organizations put together many different types of events – perhaps a civic organization whose leadership I was able to share corporate or social responsibility with, or even a church organization that was spearheading some volunteer work or sale. Regardless of which type of organization was leading the event, or whatever type of event it would be, regretfully, there would always be a time when the organizers would take a look at the audience, and it would always be the same sad scenario: only half the audience showing up to lend a hand or express support. I always saw less than the number targeted would heed the call for support.

This same scenario would always prompt the same astonished questions and the same soul-searching conundrum. Didn't we give it our all to prepare for this event? Didn't we decide on a theme, define our audience, research venues, and research catering? Didn't we create a budget? Didn't we manage and promote it? Didn't we set up an event page? Didn't we send out invitations? Didn't we harness untapped potential? Didn't we maximize time and resources, even used personal supplies and dipped into our own pockets so that the event would actually happen?

Yes, we did all these and much more. So why? Why were the seats half empty? Where were those people who had promised to come? Where was the reinforcement and the backing that was supposed to be given to the assembly?

The answer to that, I believe, would be similar to what Owl said to Pooh. "It's not us. It's them."

What those dreadful experiences taught me was that I could never expect to depend on people who have varying degrees of task and trustworthiness. A leader cannot demand that particular kind of dedication from the members of the team they are working with, much less from others who are not part of the team. A team member gives their word, but sometimes things happen and that member does not fulfill their promise. Much less can be expected from someone who is not even part of the team. They may be part of the umbrella organization but are not direct members of the organizing or managing committee.

No matter how hard we try, we cannot guarantee that our expectations of a full-house at our event will be met. A lot goes into the planning of big events so it is understandable to be a little (or even very) upset when people do not show up.

This is the "bad" in the "good", the answer to the question posed in the title of this chapter.

Consider, say, the more-than-three-hundred Overseas Filipino Workers (OFW) internally housed within the jurisdiction of the Philippine Consulate in the United Arab Emirates. A series of mental health programs had been prepared for them, i.e., from mental health awareness to provision of specific psychosocial services. Psychological first aid would be given to those suffering from mental health problems and would be on the verge of hurting themselves.

Despite the numerous events that had been set up to assist OFWs in their diverse needs and situations, and to maintain their links with the Consulate, venues and functions halls that had been reserved for gatherings and clinics were seldom well-attended. It was often disheartening to experience that after all the efforts expended and all the various systems put into place, only half of the expected audience would actually turn up.

One could always ponder on the question, "Why did people still find excuses not to attend?"

The answer? Leaders should never set the bar too high. Expectations for the best outcome must be set, yes, but they must also be ready for something else, i.e., that inevitability of half of those invited not making an appearance.

It's all too human to be disappointed with some turnouts that may not line up with our expectations but I believe that we need to come to terms with these disappointments if we want to be effective leaders.

According to Bags of Love (www.bagsoflove.co.uk), it will take quite a while to wrap our heads around this and answer the question "Why?" after that moment of disbelief when, at the hour of the event, people are not queueing up at the entrances.

This initial shock and disappointment will wear off and the moment of denial will set in. It is not that people aren't coming. It's just that they aren't there *yet*.

However, when people finally come (but they do in a trickle), guilt sets in. Is it our fault that people aren't here? Is there something else that we failed to do or something that we did wrong?

Then we get mad. They promised that they would come, didn't they? How dare they not show up? Then we feel alone and abandoned.

But I believe that it is time to face the fact that people did not come to the event, and not torture ourselves with these nagging and pointless questions – so that we could move on. We must celebrate regardless. Celebrate those who *did* come. At the end of the day, we realize that those who sat with us, watched our every move, hung on to our every word, and thought of ways they could also apply in their lives what we have been talking about – these are the people who truly mattered.

We need to talk to them, listen to them. With the hall half empty, it will be easier to move around and shake hands and try to get to know people better. Conversations will be more personal and answers to any and all questions can be delivered right away to a smaller audience. This is the "good" in the "bad".

I'm emphasizing this point at this juncture because I've learned a very good thing. It's this: *My sense of purpose must not falter.* Being given a smaller audience than expected should not matter to me, or to any leader. I should not feel upset, hesitate or lose determination because people in my environment do not have the same level of commitment as I have. I should not fall back from accomplishing my set purposes. I have set my purposes so I must deliver – with or without an audience, whether the auditorium is full-packed or half-empty.

There is one other factor to consider: the quality of the people who did come, those willing to spend time with me, to share what they know, their expertise. Shared time and know-how are most valuable when brought out into the light, talked about, and learned from. They become appreciated.

No matter how small the number was, *the full potential of the team could be harnessed by appreciating their value* and by motivating them to continue what they have started and to pursue the things that they have set their hearts and minds on. In other words, not only is the team strengthened but, more importantly, so is the leader of the team.

A burning piece of wood, when taken away from the bonfire, sizzles until the flame is extinguished. But when it is put back into the bonfire, put back with the other burning pieces of wood, the resulting fire becomes as strong as ever.

Therefore, that sense of purpose that is innate in the heart and mind of the leader of the community should be directed towards other members of the community. One could learn from the other and influence the other. Thus, they both begin to share the same strong flame of commitment.

Powerful insights can be drawn from Denis E. Waitley, author of "Seeds of Greatness" and "The Winner's Edge". Regarding the half-filled room, he advised us to not dwell on what went wrong but to focus instead on what to do next and to spend our energies on moving forward toward finding the answers to more important questions. We also, he said, ought to "learn from the past, set vivid, detailed goals for the future, and live in the only moment of time over which you have any control: now". Commitment is that turning point in our lives when we seize the moment and convert it into opportunities that alter our destinies.

In other words, let us not pay heed anymore to the number of people who did not come – who they were and what their reasons were for not coming. Those projected numbers that we had in mind? Let us forget about them. Overthinking things will only cause us unnecessary stress. What we need to do is give value back to the people who paid attention to us and to our message.

It would be perhaps understandable if we, at a certain moment of immaturity, meet the people who did not attend, to further question them and insist on knowing the reason for their absence. That would be a rather awkward situation for both leader and absentee, and is not to be advised, as it would not be a fruitful conversation.

Guilt could rear its head, as it sometimes does. "Why didn't I have that opportunity to sustain the height of expectations, the high end of quality that they needed to give?" However, at the end of the day, again, it will always be maturity on our part to appreciate the commitment of the people who did come. To be more proactive is to demonstrate a sense of willingness to accept what happened and then move forward.

Ken Blanchard, the American author of The One-Minute Manager, business consultant, and motivational speaker, is credited with saying, "There's a difference between interest and commitment. When you're interested in something, you do it only when it's convenient. When you're committed to something, you accept no excuses, only results."That would be the essential link between community engagement and community leadership. If we want to stand the test of time, we do *not* look for/to people who do *not* perform, who are simply interested. We look for/to people who are committed and are deeply engaged.

> We need to give more encouragement to the 'special breed of givers'. Before we know it, that kind of commitment that we see in them will even strengthen us in a way that is consistent with our personal level of commitment and, at the same time, enrich our very sense of purpose.

Moreover, we don't look for people who are weak in their sense of commitment and purpose. We must appreciate those who choose to be present, who give more of themselves to the cause than others are willing to do. We need to give more encouragement to this special breed of givers. Before we know it, that kind of commitment that we see in them will even strengthen us in a way that is consistent with our personal level of commitment and, at the same time, enrich our very sense of purpose.

The level of commitment is something that we probably miscalculated in the process of observing people around us, and this too high (or too low) an expectation affects the quality of our community engagement, of our community involvement, and of the action plan that we wish to introduce to the community. We learn from our mistakes and we promise to do better the next time.

I have talked about commitment in this chapter. If kindness is the heart of community engagement, commitment then would be that ingredient that fuels community leadership. Once we have ignited that strong commitment in ourselves, nothing can defeat our sense of purpose. The entirety of my community engagements which started way back in high school continued to college, and then permeated my professional career in many ways, with commitment fueling the journey.

A sense of purpose is something that gave me that power to lead. Reaching deeply into ourselves, we realize that we have something to offer to the world. We were not created in the likeness and image of God just to exist and do whatever we want to do. Yes, we empower ourselves but for what purpose?

This is the reason why I always emphasize my personal adage: The power to give is the ability to be kind. If there is such a thing as a duality of effectiveness, kindness is one half of this duality, and commitment, the other half. The power that fuels kindness is our strong commitment to the cause if we want to be part of it.

Organizations engage in corporate social responsibility and build stakeholder value by coming up with practices and policies aimed at positively influencing the world. One could be a hero in a solo fight, in a personal undertaking, or one could be part of a team. Either way, giving back to the community would be their ultimate goal and purpose.

## Reflections

Key Insights: Draw from this Chapter your major takeaways.

1. ________________________________________

________________________________________

________________________________________

2. ________________________________________

________________________________________

________________________________________

3. ________________________________________

________________________________________

________________________________________

Recount events in your life related to the Key Insights.

1. ________________________________________

________________________________________

________________________________________

2. ________________________________________

________________________________________

________________________________________

3. ________________________________________

________________________________________

________________________________________

How can these Key Insights guide you and prepare you for life's present and future challenges?

1. ____________________________________________

____________________________________________

____________________________________________

2. ____________________________________________

____________________________________________

____________________________________________

3. ____________________________________________

____________________________________________

____________________________________________

## Chapter 8

# A Measure of Leadership

"

**Not every person with ability is dependable, and not every dependable person has the ability.**

*Billy McConnel*

In our 2018 travel for a community work, Mercy and Rodessa, well-known Filipino community leaders in Mozambique woke up early one morning, excited for what the day would bring. My fellow speakers from the United Arab Emirates – Rachel, Cristina, and Art, came over to conduct series of classroom management, emotional intelligence, mental health, and financial literacy, among other life skills trainings. The more than 300 educators from Mozambique were the beneficiary of the training programs and everyone in the small village was overjoyed upon learning that we would be coming to train the teachers of Mozambique, on the invitation of Mercy who was already working there.

According to UNESCO (2020), Mercy and Rodessa's Mozambique, a small state in Africa, is a multilingual country with over 20 languages spoken. While knowledge of Portuguese is vital to access state services, a comprehensive understanding of local languages is crucial for community participation. Considering only 17% of the population speaks Portuguese as their first language, incorporating local languages into adult education and creating opportunities for bilingual teaching is key to providing relevant and inclusive lifelong learning for all (en.unesco.org.news).

Not only Mercy and Rodessa, but their entire village were very eager to meet us who would be coming from halfway across the globe on a philanthropic mission. Usually, guests were greeted by a specially selected group. However, that was not the case this time. No garlands of flowers and ribbons were prepared for us, and no tarpaulins were hanging from trees for everyone to see. Instead, the whole village was the welcoming committee.

Simple huts with thatched roofs and conical foundations, made of readily available materials such as mud, cow dung, bricks, or grass, awaited us. Simple dishes made of starchy root tuber products filled with meat, fish, and various spices and herbs, alongside some stew, were served.

That, dear Reader, is a little background on the African state that I and my colleagues had the privilege and the honor of being invited to as trainers in life skills, personal development, and community leadership. I met Mercy and Rodessa, who were educators and administrators of their own schools. They shared with me their hopes and dreams for their village – to have a better and responsible teaching workforce; and their country – to have a peaceful environment.

My team, Rachel, Art, Cristina, and I flew to Mozambique intending to share with the locals and guests alike our expertise and direct know-how on how to build and sustain successful communities. We were prepared for whatever scenario was in store for us. Since poverty rates in the country had been steadily increasing, especially in rural areas, primarily as a result of natural disasters, decreasing foreign direct investments, and civil unrest due to military attacks, we did not expect much. We were very careful not to expect much. This is where dependability comes into the picture.

I believe that once you are genuine about your intentions to lead, you do not need an audience to feel that you are appreciated. Dependability speaks volumes about what authentic leadership should be, even though there is no public acclaim. You remain true to your call of service. You primarily give your full support with or without the acknowledgment or appreciation of other people.

Imagine this scenario. Life Coach X is a big in the area of community leadership. Yes, he participates in goal-setting, in getting rid of unhelpful beliefs, and in de-escalating anxiety and stress. He supports in fulfilling dreams and in carrying out visions and missions. However, if he does all these only because he wants to be the center of attention, to gain fame, to be talked about in certain circles, or for public relation value in the news or on social media, then he is not true to form with regard to true intentions of community leadership.

> **A bloated ego defeats the very core of authentic leadership and the real essence of genuine community engagement. It is superficial, ephemeral and people will eventually realize that it is not genuine, as it is not what people hope to see in true leadership.**

Life Coach X's pursuits and undertaking are all accomplished for the wrong reasons! This I know: the ego cannot be bigger than the vision we ought to fulfill.

A bloated ego, for me, defeats the very core of authentic leadership and the real essence of a genuine community engagement. It is skin deep, an act carried out in that moment of giving something away, e.g. financially, but the act itself cannot be sustained. It is superficial, ephemeral and people will eventually realize that it is not genuine, as it is not what people hope to see in true leadership.

The Hawthorne Studies (opentexbc.ca) in 1920s, focused primarily on how human behavior and relations affect organizational performance and suggested that employees perform better when they feel singled out for special attention or feel that management is concerned about employee welfare in the United States of America. The pride that comes from special attention motivates workers to increase their productivity. Supervisors who allow employees to have some control over their situation appeared to further increase the workers' motivation.

> Without a shadow of a doubt, I would say, "You are measured by the truthfulness of what you're saying, by the authenticity of what you're doing." Borrowing from the idea of the recency effect, whenever people have their performance appraisals at the end of the year when they have first-hand information that they are being evaluated, they put their guard up and toe the line very carefully so as not to make mistakes. This is why anomalous scores happen in performance management reviews.

People do more because their immediate supervisor happens to be there. And they're being watched. They know that they're being watched and, therefore, they do more, and try to perform better and come up with better results. More effort is exerted towards the end of the process rather than at the beginning. An anomaly happens afterwards. This is what's termed as the "recency effect", which is an error in evaluation. The recency effect is a cognitive bias in which those items, ideas, or arguments that came last are remembered more clearly than those that came first (sciencedirect.com).

This, however, is not genuine leadership. Exerting effort towards the end, creating an impression to be noticed, is fake and is not bona fide community engagement. This action is inauthentic since it is being done for the sake of approval and appraisal.

Without a shadow of a doubt, I would say, "You are measured by the truthfulness of what you're saying, by the authenticity of what you're doing." Borrowing from the idea of the recency effect, whenever people have their performance appraisals at the end of the year when they have first-hand information that they are being evaluated, they put their guard up and toe the line very carefully so as not to make mistakes. This is why anomalous scores happen in performance management reviews. Legitimate community leaders refrain from accepting the authority and conforming to rules presented by this type of person.

So, dear Reader, give me Mozambique any day and any time and I shall show you what genuine intentions and authentic leadership are and should be. To me, the name Mozambique spells D-E-P-E-N-D-A-B-I-L-I-T-Y. I believe that my trip to Mozambique was a testing ground for unquestionable intentions and authentic governance.

While in Mozambique, my team and I knew that we were in for hard work and, perhaps, a lot of misunderstanding, too, due to language and cultural differences. The space was limited. The environment was not ideal by some standards and, honestly, we dreaded the end result after three days. There were more than three hundred participants. Some were Mozambicans, some Indians, some Pakistanis, and more than 80% were Filipinos.

> I'm proud to say that honesty and sincerity, straightforwardness and reliability, truth and credibility were all passwords to having a Mozambique mindset during the time that we were there. This experience and all the humbling lessons it taught me made me realize that participating in true community engagement bares one's soul, leaves one bereft of pride and self-service, and eliminates any cravings for the limelight and recognition. What is left is the faithful and frank rendering of one's occupation and craft.

However, the visiting team did not mind where we would be welcomed, where we would work, where we would teach, where we would have our meals, or where we would sleep. And that made all the difference! Truth to tell, we did not have conference rooms, sleek projectors, rotating chairs, and painted tables. We conducted training in somebody's backyard. The floor was dried, hardened mud, mixed with sand, clay, and a portion, properly cemented. Our projector was a rusty old one and our screen was a simple, white linen cloth! But we truly did not mind. In reality, our expectations were exceeded.

In the three days that we were there to teach and train, we intended to be truly present – physically, mentally, emotionally – to be one with the people, one with our audience, to inquire of them, and to listen to what they had to say. We did not mince words with our audience and they did not mince words with us. I'm proud to say that honesty and sincerity, straightforwardness and reliability, truth and credibility were all passwords to having a Mozambique mindset during the time that we were there. This experience and all the humbling lessons it taught me made me realize that participating in true community engagement bares one's soul, leaves one bereft of pride and self-service, and eliminates any cravings for the limelight and recognition. What is left is the faithful and frank rendering of one's occupation and craft.

If acknowledgment and appreciation *do* come at the end, even without expectations, it was not because this was sought or pursued. In this instance, the community recognizes what selfless leadership truly means, recognition is given, and appreciation is received with happiness and gratitude.

> **A deep sense of purpose enjoins the character trait of dependability. One would have to be consistent with one's behavior and with the "whys" and "wherefores" of this life to be dependable. "Depend" + "able". Two terms say it all. Then the communities we are engaged in may perhaps label us "dependable" if we can be there, with them, for them, during good times and in bad.**

At the end of the training program, I'm very happy to report that the audience described us as "a most dependable team", seeing that our intentions to teach, train, support, and share knowledge were genuine. The training programs that we taught were "doable, viable, and practicable", and "can be sustained through life's ups and downs", some of the feedback statements said. Mercy and

Rodessa said that her village would be very honored to welcome us back!

Our difficult experiences in life teach us that only real hardship can effect true stewardship. Life is hard and people constantly react to whatever is thrown at them. Victor Frankl has been attributed to have said: "Between stimulus and response, there is a space. In that space is our power to choose our response. In our response lies our growth and our freedom." That space urges us to honor the pause as a time to reflect on our next choice, action, or response.

We can choose to be dependable or not, to be true to our intentions or not, to value our audience or our communities or not. To see through their pains and anguish, discomfort, and distress, and feel all these would be the right thing to do if we were to be true to our inner calling and mission. Hopefully, we will not zero in on our egos, our self-assuredness, our self-importance, and vanity.

> **Dependability is such a palpable and observable trait that radiates through the light of community engagements. We are content that we are our own audience and can remain true and heed our calling and passion. We give our time, our resources, our expertise, our gifts - freely and without reservation, without thinking about any reward, but wholly with intentionality, meaning, and purpose.**

Our task as community engagers and life coaches is never vainglorious. It is humble modest, and unpretentious. If one wants to shine on social media brag of his name and accomplishments, then being a committed community leader should be the thing furthest from his mind. If he tells himself and others, "I am a good leader" and puts himself above others, then he defeats the very purpose for which the phrase "servant leadership" has been coined.

A deep sense of purpose enjoins the character trait of dependability. One would have to be consistent with one's behavior and with the whys and wherefores of this life to be dependable. "Depend" + "able". Two terms say it all. We build upon our abilities, our resources, our talents. We build up our protective walls high, brick upon brick upon brick. Then the communities we are engaged in may perhaps label us "dependable" if we can be there, with them, for them, during good times and in bad.

Dependability is such a palpable and observable trait that radiates through the light of community engagements, so that even without people to appreciate what we are doing, we still do things, we still act, and do not stop. We are content that we are our own audience and that we can remain true and heed our calling and passion. We give our time, our resources, our expertise, our gifts – freely and without reservation, without thinking about any reward, but wholly with intentionality, meaning, and purpose.

This, for me, is dependability, one of the true measures of leadership.

## Reflections

Key Insights: Draw from this Chapter your major takeaways.

1. ______________________________________________

______________________________________________

______________________________________________

2. ______________________________________________

______________________________________________

______________________________________________

3. ______________________________________________

______________________________________________

______________________________________________

Recount events in your life related to the Key Insights.

1. ______________________________________________

______________________________________________

______________________________________________

2. ______________________________________________

______________________________________________

______________________________________________

3. ______________________________________________

______________________________________________

______________________________________________

How can these Key Insights guide you and prepare you for life's present and future challenges?

1. ______________________________________________

______________________________________________

______________________________________________

2. ______________________________________________

______________________________________________

______________________________________________

3. ______________________________________________

______________________________________________

______________________________________________

Chapter 9

# Wounded but Unbroken

Love, connection, and acceptance are your birthright.

*Dr. Kristin Neff*

When you begin to touch your heart or let your heart be touched, you begin to discover that it's bottomless, that it doesn't have any resolution, that this heart is huge, vast, and limitless. You begin to discover how much warmth and gentleness there is, as well as how much space.

PEMA CHÖDRÖN

“There isn't enough foil!” I complained to myself. “Hmmph! The room is still a bit bright!”

I added more strips of foil to the wall so that no streak of light could penetrate. Thick curtains instead of the old, flimsy ones, were hung, to ward off the cold and prevent any additional light from entering the room.

Hallucination, I believe, took a momentary grip on me, when I decided to shut myself up in my room, avoiding contact with anyone or anything. It was February 2021, the second year of the dreaded coronavirus (COVID-19) pandemic, and I had tested positive for the virus. Alas, in my case, there was a co-morbidity, namely, diabetes. Not long after, after shutting myself up and shunning everyone, depression began to set in.

”

One day I was contemplating my illnesses and the next, I was already entertaining depressing thoughts in my mind. This depression was triggered by two major illnesses happening together, which were accompanied by inactivity, social withdrawal, loss of concentration, and sleep disturbances.

Looking back on it now, and with the added benefit of hindsight, I say that this spirit of severe melancholy came without warning. One day I was contemplating my illnesses and the next, I was already entertaining depressing thoughts in my mind. This depression was triggered by two major illnesses happening together, which were accompanied by inactivity, social withdrawal, loss of concentration, and sleep disturbances. At that time, I resigned myself to the feeling of simply letting everyone and everything go, that what I had been feeling was "normal" and since others experienced such feelings, I was allowed to experience them, too.

I started to avoid people, to withdraw socially. I did not participate in any social and community-based activities, even though they were all delivered online. I canceled all my webinars, and was not open to talking about my feelings with family or friends, let alone with a doctor or a mental health professional. I stayed in my room of darkness, literally, for three months. I held myself captive, incarcerated by my own choice while suffering from the effects of Covid-19 and diabetes. I engulfed myself in the darkness that bewildered those around me, including my nine-year-old son, who asked, "Daddy, why aren't you going out anymore?"

I felt troubled, helpless, hopeless. I was heavy, sluggish, errant in my thoughts, wretched in my behavior. I became hyper sensitive about the littlest things, complaining and finding fault in everything. The phrases "community leader" and "servant leadership" were the farthest things from my mind in those three months that I was in self-exile, an excommunicado from the rest of the world.

Dear Reader, my boundaries had come tumbling down, you see? The walls that I had meticulously constructed brick by *brick by brick* for the last twenty years had finally collapsed, and I succumbed to compassion fatigue, followed by depression.

I felt troubled, helpless, hopeless. I could not even bring myself to get out of bed! I was heavy, sluggish, errant in my thoughts, wretched in my behavior. I felt sad and empty without knowing why, and was always extremely tired but not really doing any physical activity at all. I became hyper sensitive about the littlest things, complaining and finding fault in everything. As a result, my family had a most difficult time caring for me and trying to restore me to health. The phrases "community leader" and "servant leadership" were the farthest things from my mind in those three months that I was in self-exile, an *excommunicado* from the rest of the world.

Another very odd thing happened to me. I overindulged in food. I realized soon enough that I should not only be socially distancing myself from other people. I must socially distance myself from the pantry and the refrigerator as well! According to Jean Illsley-Clarke, overindulgence is "giving too much, for too long, too soon." That was me, for three months! No wonder I gained so much weight even while suffering from Covid-19 and diabetes!

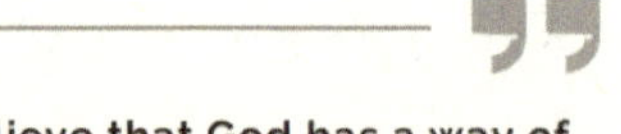

**I believe that God has a way of telling us where we are and what we have done so far with our lives and His way of intervening and showing us if anything is amiss comes in many forms. Whatever shape this warning or counsel may take, we must stop and pay attention (even midway), take an objective look, assess the situation, then implement meaningful solutions.**

My two illnesses severely restricted me, forcing me to stay only in my bedroom all of the time (and the room did not get enough light since I sealed it up in foil and thick curtains). I was severely limited and measured in my physical activities, on top of which I overindulged myself in food and choosing to ignore my family. Self-pity, coupled with stress resulted in depression.

I was not aware that I was even falling into the abyss of depression. I had downplayed the signs and symptoms. How could I be depressed? No way! When I always discussed with people what depression was and the key role that mental health played in the lives of leaders? Wasn't I the speaker at a national conference that featured the issues of mental health, depression, and suicide? Didn't we distinguish at that very conference male from female brain chemistry, hormones, and life experiences? And didn't we agree that mental health issues could overlap with medical conditions, and that professional help was the key to an accurate diagnosis and appropriate treatment?

Indeed, depression should not have happened to me had I listened to some voices and heeded some counsel. I believe that God has a way of telling us where we are and what we have done so far with our lives and His way of intervening and showing us if anything is amiss comes in many forms. It could be our own bodies crying out for help. It could be friends and family warning us about the dire consequences of fatigue and overworking. Whatever shape this warning or counsel may take, we must stop and pay attention (even midway), take an objective look, assess the situation, then implement meaningful solutions.

Most often than not, we are able to stop just in the nick of time, without prejudicing any important area, regretting any misstep along the way, or making any wrong decision. This would be the right time to take that unquestionably critical respite for the healing of body and mind. Then after this much-needed break is done, we regroup, rethink, and rewire for the next challenges.

Leaders truly love serving others. We spearhead activities that are, most often than not, larger than ourselves, bigger than all our collective expectations. Our energies seem endless; our time, immutable; our resources, unlimited. To humanity, we give and we give until there is nothing more to give.

But isn't this what leadership is about? What our true calling awaits us to do? How community leadership should be practiced?

But how could we serve if we've become bone-dry? Completely reduced to the barest of our elements? Utterly depleted in all our energies and stamina, time, and resources?

Most often than not, we are able to stop just in the nick of time, without prejudicing any important area, regretting any misstep along the way, or making any wrong decision. This would be the right time to take that unquestionably critical respite for the healing of body and mind. Then after this much-needed break is done, we regroup, rethink, and rewire for the next challenges.

And, yes, fatigued, very fatigued. Perhaps, as leaders, we are always going to fall a little short, as we always seem to push ourselves just a little too hard, for just that little bit too long, until we are forced to pay attention. It's a learning process, looking after ourselves.

Indeed, self-compassion is about serving others, about being unconditional with our concern for people. However, we miss one important ingredient in this selfless love and devotion.

In our all-out giving, we forget that we, too, should always be constantly replenished and refreshed to be able to give. When we talk about, say, mental health programs befitting the community, it is our own state of mental health and well-being that we should be caring about first *before* we even think of lending a helping hand. This is not selfishness. Far from it. It is simply the most logical thing to do. We will never be able to give away what we did not have in the first place.

> **Self-care is essential if we want to serve others better. It means taking an active role in protecting our own sense of well-being and happiness, especially during periods of stress. Self-care goes hand-in-hand with self-compassion. When done with intentionality, both self-care and self-compassion make us slow down to even help improve our self-love and self-kindness in the long run.**

Self-care is essential if we want to serve others better. It means taking an active role in protecting our own sense of well-being and happiness, especially during periods of stress. Self-care goes hand-in-hand with self-compassion. When done with intentionality, both self-care and self-compassion make us slow down and take fewer steps for these reasons: to make us aware of what is going on with our bodies and minds, to help boost our immune system, and to even help improve our self-love and self-kindness in the long run.

Self-compassion comes as a vital toolkit used to uplift oneself so that other people can also be lifted. Only when we possess the power to manage our energies - physical, mental, emotional, and, to some extent, social, can we be a source of strength and inspiration for others to emulate.

According to Ana Sandoiu (2018), self-care, self-love, and self-compassion might actually be needed most by leaders like us, who try to give all, and be all, "those of us who work too hard and are constantly striving to surpass ourselves and grasp the shape-shifting phantasm of perfection." Being too hard on ourselves because we are driven by this overwhelming desire to excel or to prove ourselves, we tend to do everything right, "all the time".

Depletion of energy and resources results in this phenomenon of over-giving. Exhaustion and collapse, or simply burnout, inevitably takes place, and the leader, suddenly, is nowhere to be found! When asked where he is or what has happened, no one can answer because the leader has hidden himself away, and has broken off from all his social media entanglements. The answer? He has given much too much away without taking the precaution to first replenish and refresh himself.

> **Imperfection is part of the shared human experience—we're not alone in our suffering. Often, when something goes wrong, we look in the mirror and don't like what we see—we feel very isolated at that moment, as if everyone else has these perfect lives and it's just us who are flawed and defective. When we remember that imperfection is part of the shared human experience, we can actually feel more connected to people in those moments.**

Dr. Kristin Neff (2003) has operationalized self-compassion as consisting of three elements: self-kindness, common humanity, and mindfulness. In a *Greater Good* interview by Jason Marsh (2013), Neff clarified these three.

The first one is self-kindness, as opposed to self-judgment. A lot of times when we suffer, we just take a very cold attitude toward ourselves. So self-compassion involves being warm and supportive—actively soothing ourselves—as opposed to being cold and judging ourselves.

The second part is remembering that imperfection is part of the shared human experience—that we're not alone in our suffering. Often, when something goes wrong, we look in the mirror and don't like what we see—we feel very isolated at that moment, as if everyone else has these perfect lives and it's just us who are flawed and defective. When we remember that imperfection is part of the shared human experience, we can actually feel more connected to people in those moments.

If we are not mindfully aware that we are suffering, if we are just repressing our pain or ignoring it or getting lost in problem-solving, we can't give ourselves compassion. We need to say, "Wait a second. This hurts. This is really hard. This is a moment where I need compassion." If we don't want to be somewhere, if it's too painful to go there, we have to admit this and not go there. This way, we can be compassionate to ourselves.

The third component is mindfulness. If we are not mindfully aware that we are suffering, if we are just repressing our pain or ignoring it or getting lost in problem-solving, we can't give ourselves compassion. We need to say, "Wait a second. This hurts. This is *really* hard. This is a moment where I need compassion." If we don't want to be somewhere, if it's too painful to go there, we have to admit this and not go there. This way, we can be compassionate to ourselves.

My own depression "episode" during the pandemic was an enlightening experience for me. It proved that I was exempt from the risks and dangers that plagued a leader. I saw my own fallibility and vulnerability, my imperfection and inadequacy, my humaneness. I saw myself in a much clearer light, recognized my flaws, and admitted that leaders are not immune to being unwell. I believe that, in those three months when I was depressed, I acted toward myself in a way I never wanted others to act toward me.

In one of my community engagements in Abu Dhabi, the capital of Emirates on May 1, 2022, in my parting words, I said that in leading change, we must care for one that's truly important: ourselves. No one could really take care of us but us. Are we ready to lead? Are we physically, emotionally, mentally, and socially able to lead? By asking ourselves the question "What do I need?" – and listening mindfully to the answer and accepting the honesty of the answer – we can be on our way toward healing and true community leadership.

> Mental health is like a pendulum. Our well-being may swing from being good and being empowered on one end, to then being heavy and depressed on the other.We become stressed, yes, but it does not end in stress. Sadly, this further develops into depression and mood swings of varying degrees. It is impossible to feel elation and a bubbly sensation, and guilt and despair all in one pendulum swing.

It is a noble task to become a community leader. The way we handle change as we move on to a post-pandemic world, for example, determines the extent of our contribution to the world. Our legacy is indeed distinguished by our passion to lead without conditions. Defined lines, however, should tell us very clearly if we should even continue if issues on mental health and well-being are not comprehensively discussed in terms of what is acceptable social behavior.

All of us want to contribute to the betterment of the community. But how can we do that unless we are whole ourselves? Again, we cannot give away something that we do not have. Our personal struggles often bring us to the point of physical difficulties, illnesses, and depression. Eventually, what happens to us is not a match to what we aim for. We fall below the bar and do not make it a high standard.

Mental health is like a pendulum. Our well-being may swing from being good and being empowered on one end, to then being heavy and depressed on the other. We become stressed, yes, but it does not end in stress. Sadly, this further develops into depression and mood swings of varying degrees. It is impossible to feel elation and a bubbly sensation, and guilt and despair all in one pendulum swing.

> Community leaders, human as they are, are not infallible, nor are they indispensable. We know how it is to fully lead and we can stand before a crowd, deliver the message without batting an eyelash, and still be true to our core values and principles. Self-compassion, self-kindness, common humanity, and mindfulness all bring us to the realization that we are but earthly being who fail and make mistakes.

"Depression is not sadness. Its emotional paraplegia. It's an emptiness and a numbness that consumes every bit of who you are. Everything you do. Everywhere you go. It suffocates you and no matter what you do or where you go and how good you feel at that particular moment, there is always a part of your brain that keeps the "depression switch" on. You cannot run from it ... Nothing feels like everything, and everything is too much. Too much sadness, too much anxiety, restlessness, exhaustion, too much lack of motivation, too much empathy for others, and, truthfully, not enough empathy for yourself." (Bailey Harvey, *The Depression Pendulum that Swings Back and Forth*, July 29, 2021).

Mental health issues have grown to such huge proportions that the United Nations has included in its Sustainable Development Goals and Agenda 2030 the promotion of mental health and prevention strategies for people needing help and assistance. To this goal, it intends as human rights instrument an explicit social development dimension. It reaffirms that all people with all types of disabilities including mental health conditions and psychosocial disabilities must enjoy all human rights and fundamental freedoms. It clarifies how all domains of rights apply to persons with disabilities on an equal basis with others. It also identifies areas where adaptations must be made for people with disabilities to effectively exercise their rights, and where protection of rights must be reinforced.

Community leaders, human as they are, are not infallible, nor are they indispensable. We know how it is to fully lead and we can stand before a crowd, deliver the message without batting an eyelash, and still be true to our core values and principles. Self-compassion, self-kindness, common humanity, and mindfulness all bring us to the realization that we are but earthly being who fail and make mistakes.

Most depressed individuals do not know they are depressed more than 60% of the time. Even mental health advocates are not exempted from being stressed out. The way, therefore, to combat depression and other mental health issues is through social awareness. By this, we mean creating a social awareness campaign to spread positive mental health and well-being, i.e. doing the research, choosing the right date for the campaign, finding the target audience, crafting the message, securing sponsors and ambassadors, using multiple channels, optimizing donation sites, etc.

We look back at times with pain and we recognize it as such pain – but we do not linger there. Sometimes we need to look at the past squarely in the eye, and accept it as such but we must move on, and, if we can, we forgive. Only then can we start the healing process in our lives. To heal is to look deep into ourselves, what things we must maintain, and what to give up.

Being aware also means that we know exactly what we need to do, and are careful about things to avoid, things that are better left unsaid or undone that could only lead to negativity in physical and mental health.

Anything that could impede us in our quest toward self-realization and community leadership must be avoided at all costs. We look back at times with pain and we recognize it as such pain – but we do not linger there. Sometimes we need to look at the past squarely in the eye, and accept it as such but we must move on, and, if we can, we forgive. Only then can we start the healing process in our lives. To heal is to look deep into ourselves, what things we must maintain, and what to give up.

People, indeed, are our support system. We live different lives but leaders have similar roles to play. Our families serve as our inspiration and motivation since we are all sons and daughters.

People, however, are also our main source of stress. A multiplicity of roles creates a vast array of conflicts and stress triggers. Growth is painful, but the alternative to growth – being stuck somewhere, somehow – would never justify an attempt to halt the movement or action happening naturally in life.

> **We look back at times with pain and we recognize it as such pain – but we do not linger there. Sometimes we need to look at the past squarely in the eye, and accept it as such but we must move on, and, if we can, we forgive. Only then can we start the healing process in our lives. To heal is to look deep into ourselves, what things we must maintain, and what to give up.**

On the spiritual side of things, our work may indeed be our sure reward. But there is a much surer reward from the One who finally gives it. Thinking that we deserve better than what we are receiving may not be true to the picture of true community leadership. This would not be in agreement with that picture since we work not because of expectation of a reward but for reasons of kindness and shared humanity.

The more compassionate leaders are toward people, the more compassionate they should be toward themselves. Constantly finding fault within ourselves diminishes us. It demeans and debases us. It does not afford us the growth, advancement, resilience, and the power to bounce back from all the negativity that has held us back. We fail in our mission to bravely meet challenges head-on without fear.

I say that the overarching qualification that a committed leader must have would be this: a good, honest dosage of self-compassion.

One cannot pour from an empty cup.

## Reflections

Key Insights: Draw from this Chapter your major takeaways.

1. ____________________________________________

____________________________________________

____________________________________________

2. ____________________________________________

____________________________________________

____________________________________________

3. ____________________________________________

____________________________________________

____________________________________________

Recount events in your life related to the Key Insights.

1. ____________________________________________

____________________________________________

____________________________________________

2. ____________________________________________

____________________________________________

____________________________________________

3. ____________________________________________

____________________________________________

____________________________________________

How can these Key Insights guide you and prepare you for life's present and future challenges?

1. ______________________________

______________________________

______________________________

2. ______________________________

______________________________

______________________________

3. ______________________________

______________________________

______________________________

## Chapter 10

# Sustaining Your Momentum

"Sow a thought and you reap an action;
Sow an act and you reap a habit;
Sow a habit and you reap a character;
Sow a character and you reap a destiny."

RALPH WALDO EMERSON

MANAGEMENT
CASES
MANAGEMENT
No matter how unpleasant things are, optimism sustains our momentum and steers us clear toward the right path.

"Well, can you do it?" I asked him again.

A myriad of emotions ran across the face of the young Patrol Leader. I could see what he was thinking. I could read his face. He did not utter a single word but his emotions were very forthcoming.

The first emotion was surprise.

"What? Me, Sir?"

The second emotion was fear.

"No, no, no! Not me. I can't do it."

The third emotion was uneasiness.

> **Optimists tend to view hardships as learning experiences or temporary setbacks. Even the most miserable day holds the promise for them that "tomorrow will probably be better." If they choose to see the brighter side in things (it is always a choice), it is because they want to experience more positive events, less stress, and greater health benefits happening in their lives.**

"The next Patrol Leader would be better at this."

The fourth emotion was gaining mastery of himself and his emotions.

Until, finally, he said out loud, "Yes, Sir. I can."

That scene took place at a Boy Scout Camp (with my best friend Cris) in the Philippines sixteen years ago, when I was a Scout Trainer asking a young Patrol Leader if he could be the overall lead in the manhunt/survival games.

Like most of us, the initial reaction to a question verifying our competence or ability would probably follow this series: surprise, fear, uneasiness, acquiescence.

The train of thought would, of course, start in our minds. Either we choose positivity (optimism, "I can do it") or negativity (pessimism, "I can't do it"). It's that simple."

According to Scott (2020), optimism is a mental attitude characterized by hope and confidence in success and a positive future. Optimists are those who expect good things to happen, whereas pessimists, on the other hand, predict unfavorable outcomes. Optimistic attitudes are linked to several benefits, including better-coping skills, lower stress levels, better physical health, and higher persistence when pursuing goals.

> In their explanatory styles, optimists explain positive events as happening because of their own actions or innate characteristics. The events are eventualities, outcomes, of who they are and what they are as human beings. They also see them as evidence that more positive things will happen in the future and in other areas of their lives.

Optimists tend to view hardships as learning experiences or temporary setbacks. Even the most miserable day holds the promise for them that "tomorrow will probably be better." If they choose to see the brighter side in things (it is always a choice), it is because they want to experience more positive events, less stress, and greater health benefits happening in their lives.

Studies in psychology revealed that optimism reflects the belief that the outcomes of events or experiences will generally be positive. Others contend, however, that this optimism is more of an explanatory style in that it resides in the way people explain the series of events.

Explanatory styles refer to how we explain the causes of particular events. Two students got the same poor grade on a test. The optimist would say, "Oh, well. I'll just do better next time. This is just one test. I did well enough in my other subjects." The pessimist would say, "I'm always a failure! Why can't I ever get it right? I'd better drop this subject before they give me a failing grade!" Here, two people have disparate perceptions of the same event. Their explanatory styles are the ways in which they explain their circumstances to themselves.

In their explanatory styles, optimists explain positive events as happening because of their own actions or innate characteristics. The events are eventualities, outcomes, of who they are and what they are as human beings. They also see them as evidence that more positive things will happen in the future and in other areas of their lives.

Conversely, they see negative events as not being their fault and happening beyond their control. They also see these occurrences as isolated incidents, not the norm, and are negative happenstances that have nothing to do with other areas of their lives or future events.

For example, if optimists could not go out because of lockdown restrictions, they were happy because they got to spend more time with family. Or if they started their career in a less than stellar way, they believed that things would only get better. JK Rowling had twelve rejections of *Harry Potter* (1997) but never stopped submitting the manuscript because she believed that it was a great story. Bloomsbury decided to accept and publish it, and it eventually sold more than 500 million copies worldwide, being translated into eighty languages, making the story the best-selling book series in history.

The father of positive psychology, Martin Seligman, defines optimism as reacting to problems with a sense of confidence and high personal ability, believing that optimism exists on a continuum. He worked on a classification manual called "Character Strengths and Virtues" that focuses on what can go right instead of what can go wrong. He claims this manual to be the positive counterpart of the Diagnostic and Statistical Manual of Mental Disorders (DSM). While the DSM highlights the "insanities", Seligman's character manual offers a review of the traits that influence "sanity".

> **Optimism is empowering, inspiring, and uplifting. So much so that in community leadership in the corporate world, optimists are more likely to see failure or negative experiences as temporary, rather than permanent.**

Pessimists think in terms of opposites in their explanatory style. They believe that the experienced world is the worst possible, i.e. things are already bad but tend to become even worse. They also believe that negative events are caused by their own mistakes or traits. They believe that one mistake means more will come, and mistakes in other areas of life are inevitable because they are the cause. They see positive events as unexpected advantages resulting from an uncertain course of events, which and probably won't happen again.

German philosopher Arthur Schopenhauer's (1788-1860) Doctrine of Pessimism answers the question "What is the meaning of life?" this way: "Sentient beings, with few exceptions, are bound to strive and suffer greatly, all without any ultimate purpose or justification, and that life is not really worth living...One's life reflects one's will, and the will (life) is an aimless, irrational, and painful drive." Profoundly pessimistic, he ended up by saying that the meaning of life is to deny it.

A pessimist would see, say, a promotion, as a lucky event that probably won't occur again, and may even worry that they'll now be under more scrutiny. Being passed over for a promotion would probably be explained as not being skilled enough. They would, therefore, expect to be passed over again.

Winston Churchill nailed it on the head when he famously said, "A pessimist sees the difficulty in every opportunity; an optimist sees the opportunity in every difficulty."

Optimism is empowering, inspiring, and uplifting. So much so that in community leadership in the corporate world, optimists are more likely to see failure or negative experiences as temporary, rather than permanent. Even if the economy is on a significant downturn, this perspective enables optimists to see more easily the possibility of turnarounds and growth because things are just temporary and they will necessarily change.

We could personalize this construct or theory, of change happening constantly by looking at specific periods in a day. A sunrise would be the specific time for us to see the light; a sunset, a frame for us to experience darkness. There is a time for us to go out and dance in the rain and celebrate, and then, again, a time to experience drought and want and grief. Likewise, Ecclesiastes 1 records the same idea. "To everything there is a season, and a time to every purpose under heaven..."

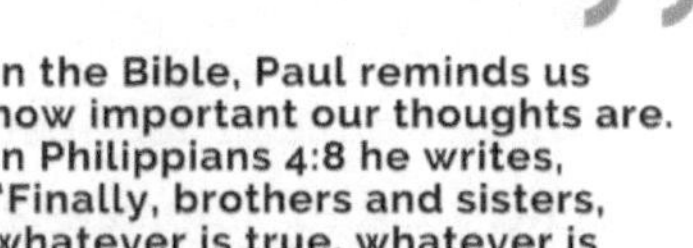

**In the Bible, Paul reminds us how important our thoughts are. In Philippians 4:8 he writes, "Finally, brothers and sisters, whatever is true, whatever is noble, whatever is right, whatever is pure, whatever is lovely, whatever is admirable — if anything is excellent or praiseworthy — think about such things." A possibility thinker dwells on these positive virtues.**

Thoughts start in the mind so we need to take precautions in guarding it well. "The mind is the battlefield," says Joyce Meyer, "a war is raging there. Worry, doubt, confusion, depression, anger, and feelings of condemnation...all these are attacks on the mind. If you suffer from negative thoughts, take heart...We must be responsible for our own thoughts and words because they produce actions." We have to equip ourselves for the battle.

Jon Hauser (2020) claims that "if you change a thought, you will change your future. Every action starts with a thought. Every attitude starts with a thought. Every destination started, not with someone else's action, but with the thought you selected."

Ralph Waldo Emerson said, "Sow a thought and you reap an action; sow an act and you reap a habit; sow a habit and you reap a character; sow a character and you reap a destiny." Our destiny is tied directly to and starts with our thoughts.

In the Bible, Paul reminds us how important our thoughts are. In Philippians 4:8 he writes, "Finally, brothers and sisters, whatever is true, whatever is noble, whatever is right, whatever is pure, whatever is lovely, whatever is admirable — if anything is excellent or praiseworthy — think about such things." A possibility thinker dwells on these positive virtues.

We want to avoid negativity and the flow of negative things in our lives, but the absorption of negativity seems to be a part of the normal flow of life. For example, there's always something that gets in the way of positive thoughts. "We should have done this", or "We should have done that", etc., etc., which can set up unrealistic expectations of ourselves and others. This involves operating by rigid rules and not allowing for flexibility.

These "should-have" statements are examples of phrases that can contribute to anxious thought patterns. These are known as Automatic Negative Thoughts (ANTs) as proposed by Dr. Timothy "Dr. Happy" Sharp (2003). ANTs are the ones that pop into our heads in response to a trigger.

They can make us feel like we have lost control of our thoughts and emotions. They fill us with feelings of self-doubt, unworthiness, sadness, frustration, fear, guilt, anger, uneasiness, and, sometimes, dread.

Roncero (2021) writes that automatic thoughts are the kind of negative self-talk that appears immediately, without us even being aware of forming a thought, in response to a certain stimulus. Each person's automatic thoughts may be different from the next person's. They are usually related to our life experiences, our fears or the messages we have internalized for years. ANTs are often irrational and negative to our mental well-being.

The good news is that there are ways to manage and control these ANTs. Indeed, no one is exempted from experiencing spiraling negative thoughts from taking control of their lives, but for people who have very strong control of their emotions, people who have high emotional intelligence, it is somewhat easier for them to be plugged into the right moment to say, "Oh, I am sucked into this spiral of negative thoughts. I must get out of here."

According to Roncero, Cognitive Behavioral Therapy (CBT) is one way to control ANTs. CBT promotes mental well-being for those whose thoughts interfere with living (those suffering from social anxiety

> **If we don't understand something, we are bound to interpret that the event that is happening is part of an emerging theme, say, of danger, that comprises fear, doubt, anxiety, and self-preservation. People thus act accordingly, producing immediate negative initial thoughts.**

and depression). Psychotherapists help identify destructive thought patterns and ANTs and change them into more constructive thought patterns.

Furthermore, Roncero suggests these steps to manage ANTs:

1. Recognize the problem.
2. Plan a solution.
3. Redirect the emotion/s.
4. Get a sense of control.
5. Take the blame off ourselves.
6. Find support.

My experience with that young Patrol Leader at the beginning of this chapter is an example of an ANT that was managed quite well. In a matter of minutes, while speaking with me, the lad went from total surprise to self-doubt to fear to uneasiness, until finally acquiescing and accepting the challenge. To no one's surprise, he led the games quite wonderfully.

If we don't understand something, we are bound to interpret that the event that is happening is part of an emerging theme, say, of danger, that comprises fear, doubt, anxiety, and self-preservation. People thus act accordingly, producing immediate negative initial thoughts. The theme "danger" is now the repetitive theme, the showrunner, that turns thoughts into paralyzing panic attacks. These insights

I have also affirmed from great community leaders from Dabarkads team; Rachel, Art, Ben, Nino, Allen, Djonde, Susan, and Sharon who would lift my spirit up when I was down while leading community-based organizations in the UAE.

Unfortunately, leaders experience these panic attacks, too. No one is indispensable. Nevertheless, managing negative thoughts that result in panic attacks and diverting them to positive, wholesome, hopeful reflection, is a skill that can be learned and mastered. Learning how to gradually take control of our emotions will bring us to a period of wakefulness and alertness. If this period happens, I believe that we will have control of our emotions at least 50% of the time.

Acquiring the mental tool of alertness is initially a little prescriptive and is the beginning of our journey toward battling ANTs. It is mind over matter. The mind is more powerful than anything else. That skill of defusing ANTs is free to anyone who wants to move out of the control of these "pests". But first, the sufferer must recognize that a problem exists and should be willing to accept the solution, which takes the form of a mental shift.

**Although pessimism can be a broad perspective that affects a general worldview, it is not a stable trait that remains unchanged throughout one's lifetime. Research suggests that optimism is a skill that can be learned. Optimism then has become a choice.**

When we find ourselves in a negative thought loop, we can consider how a mental shift can transform this experience. Bisharat (2019) suggests a few examples of mental shifts that can reduce stress and make us happier and more successful. These are: from complaining to finding out what we love about something, from doing it ourselves to asking if there is someone who can do it better or for less, from declaring that we don't have enough time to saying that we have time to do everything we need to do today.

So, when the triggers come in, and we are on the verge of being eaten by ANTs, we know what to do. We don't want to be labeled or classified as negative thinkers, or even pegged as pessimists if we are recognized community leaders, do we? We want to influence the world and influence it positively, favorably, and affirmative. I don't think we can be advocates for positive mental health if we ourselves suffer from ANTs and don't do something about them.

One could argue that pessimism can manifest as a personality trait and is at least partially influenced by genetics. According to Ericson (2013), genetic makeup can influence an individual's perception of the world by amplifying negative experiences and emotions. Pessimistic people may also be more likely to notice potential risks and experience anxiety and worry.

Although pessimism can be a broad perspective that affects a general worldview, it is not a stable trait that remains unchanged throughout one's lifetime. Research suggests that optimism is a skill that can be learned.

Optimism then has become a choice. It is more than a positive outlook. It is a vessel of hope for others, a channel of infinite possibilities for us leaders influencing the world. We can create a place where we thrive and excel, where we choose to be resilient, rather than vulnerable; courageous, rather than timid; glad, rather than despondent. We can become game-changers for ourselves and others.

Are our affirmations full of hope? Are our declarations bright, blessed, and encouraging? Are they confident and comforting? We do not want to live in a bleak, depressing world. Let us all point toward a happy outcome. Let us choose optimism.

No matter how unpleasant things are, optimism sustains our momentum and steers us clear toward the right path.

## Reflections

Key Insights: Draw from this Chapter your major takeaways.

1. ______________________________

______________________________

______________________________

2. ______________________________

______________________________

______________________________

3. ______________________________

______________________________

______________________________

Recount events in your life related to the Key Insights.

1. ______________________________

______________________________

______________________________

2. ______________________________

______________________________

______________________________

3. ______________________________

______________________________

______________________________

How can these Key Insights guide you and prepare you for life's present and future challenges?

1. ______________________________________

______________________________________

______________________________________

2. ______________________________________

______________________________________

______________________________________

3. ______________________________________

______________________________________

______________________________________

## Chapter 11

# The Power to Influence

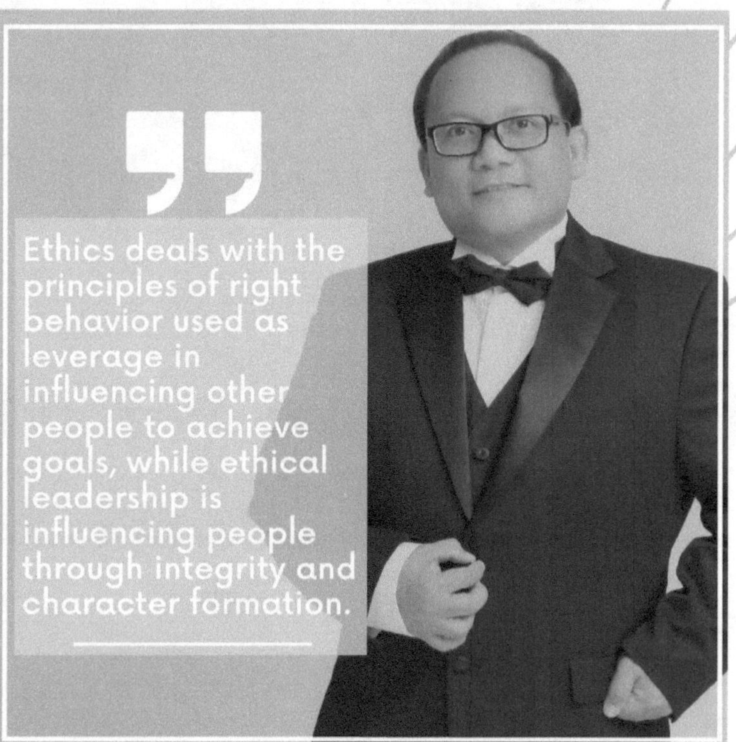

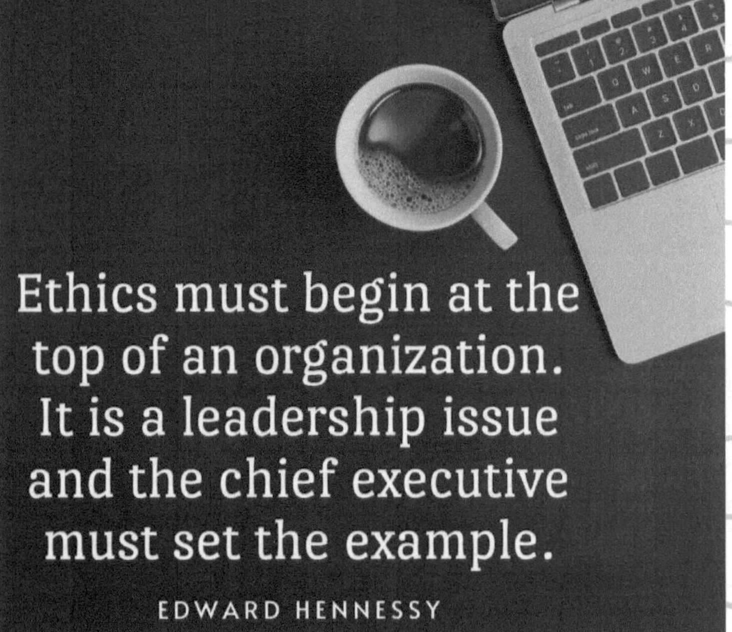
Ethics must begin at the top of an organization. It is a leadership issue and the chief executive must set the example.
EDWARD HENNESSY

> "Leaders can influence the policy, culture, and behavior of an organization. As a result, ethical leadership may be the most important lever in an ethical system designed to support ethical conduct.
>
> David Mayer

Ethical leadership is fundamentally a leadership theory employing ethical concepts as a guide to overseeing and supervising others. Since ethics deals with the principles of *right behavior* used as leverage in influencing other people to achieve goals, ethical leadership is influencing people through ethics.

Ethics isn't an idle, lifeless concept. It requires instead constant evaluation and re-evaluation to harness the benefits.

Ethical leadership is based on trust and respect. For an ethical leadership framework to work, leaders must align their ethical standards with those of the organization and ensure that an environment of openness exists. Ultimately, the practice of ethical leadership will help us move forward as a human and humane species.

Ethical leadership is based on trust and respect. For an ethical leadership framework to work, leaders must align their ethical standards with those of the organization and ensure that an environment of openness exists. Ultimately, the practice of ethical leadership will help us move forward as a human and humane species.

Dear Reader, the past two decades of my being an educator and a consultant brought me to a realization that the descriptions of ethical leadership stated above would have to include a part that says "opening oneself to the opportunity to serve unconditionally". The key words here would be "opening oneself" and "unconditionally", which both imply vulnerability and susceptibility, that leaders of this type, since they are "open" and their treatment of others "unconditional", are champions of what is right in the workplace.

However, this is my two cents' worth: opening ourselves unconditionally doesn't only make us the organization's men-of-the-hour, approximating a champion of sorts, but, sadly, sitting ducks, too, open to doubt, offense, and attack.

Others would further contend the naivety of this definition, perhaps, its lack of sophistication, of guile even, i.e. throwing oneself into a lions' den since there would be no room for self-interest and self-aggrandizement, which naturally occur in humans. It's unpretentious for the more discriminating, since this foreshadows that ethical leaders must keep their ego in check, sometimes easier said than done. Others could assume that this is stonewalling and simply putting on an act.

That is why it's lonely at the top. I think that it's happier "at the bottom" where leaders reach out to reach out to others. This is the place where the true essence of ethical leadership occurs, where servant leadership would, or could, be realized.

Ethical leadership, unnaturally occurring, and people employing this trait are sitting-ducks, even if it begins with just "a few good men" in their departments and teams – this leadership style of exhibiting morals and values sets an example of demonstrating respect and integrity in an environment of trust and accountability.

According to Luenondonk (2020), ethical leadership is considered to be one solution for creating a balance between the well-being of the subordinates and the wider community, and the organization's profitability. The theory understands the importance of trust and good relationships. In essence, modern ethical leadership theory places importance on the idea of service. The theory is therefore somewhat close to Robert Greenleaf's concept of servant leadership. Greenleaf wrote in 1977, in his famous book Servant Leadership, "Service to followers is the primary responsibility of leaders and the essence of ethical leadership".

"Ethical leaders are a rare breed in organizations," says Executive Leadership coach Dino Badilla. Often despised and unpopular, they swim against the corporate current of the easy and dishonest way of doing things. They begin as idealistic. Then they experience initiation and awakening to the reality of corporate politics and greed. They certainly need to play the game of corporate politics if they want to survive and win in their organization.

According to the 2018 Global Ethics Business Survey by the Ethics and Compliance Initiative, "employees who see evidence of proactive communication and workplace trust are fifteen times more likely to think that their company measures and rewards ethical conduct." When leaders manifest ethical conduct at any level of leadership and are rewarded for it, the entire organization notices it. Corporate culture is

> Today, organizations believe that good leadership is not merely competing, bringing profits, and creating an image, but also transforming workplaces and bringing changes to the lives of people through ethics. Morally upright leaders foster good business, encourage excellent task performance, make powerful decisions, and nurture corporate vision.

thus established on the foundations of trust, honesty, and transparency.

Themis Institute for Governance and Leadership maintains that "effective boards are those in which the strengths and expertise of the members match the needs of the organization at a given moment in time. Therefore, in today's fast-changing environment, there is a need for proactive and adaptive management of the supervisory board's composition and the role of the board members."

In conjunction with this, Tripathy (2019), in *The Power of Ethics: Rethinking Leadership Roles in Workplaces*, reported that past leadership roles in workplaces looked only into bringing profits to organizations, competing with each other, and creating a brand image come what may. The emergence of incorporating moral and ethical codes developed when both employees and leaders of organizations, both big and small, became involved got involved in unethical practices which led to tremendous loss in business and involved legal cases. Not only did the reputation of such companies become tarnished, but gradually they started losing their authenticity in the business world.

Somewhat surprisingly, perhaps, moral codes and ethical standards always existed in the organizations' policies, yet their relevance was recognized only in the twenty-first century, when business organizations began to merge and expand worldwide because of globalization, resulting in the system changing on a permanent basis.

Organizations today simply cannot compromise with unethical practices and values.

Today, organizations believe that good leadership is not merely competing, bringing profits, and creating an image, but also transforming workplaces and bringing changes to the lives of people through ethics. Studies reveal that the integration of ethics within leadership roles can bring significant benefits to workplaces. Morally upright leaders foster good business, encourage excellent task performance, make powerful decisions, and nurture corporate vision.

Robin Sharma, the author of *The Monk Who Sold His Ferrari*, and widely considered one of the top leadership and personal mastery experts and speakers in the world, once said that leadership is not like a popularity contest. It's about leaving your ego at the door. The name of the game is to lead without a title.

Another rather striking insight came from Indra Nooyi, an Indian-American business executive and former chairperson and chief executive officer of PepsiCo. In 2017, PepsiCo had a revenue of $63.53 billion. Nooyi said that "the distance between number one and number two is always a constant. If you want to improve the organization, you have to improve yourself and the organization gets pulled up with you."

Throughout Nooyi's career, she has exhibited consistent ethics and values in her pursuit of success. Nooyi embodies commitment and perseverance. She also values health, honesty, and clear communications, as well as authenticity and transparency.

Robin Sharma meant the same thing when he said, "it is only when you have mastered the art of loving yourself that you can truly love others. It's only when you have opened your own heart that you can touch the hearts of others. When you feel centered and alive, you are in a much better position to be a better person."

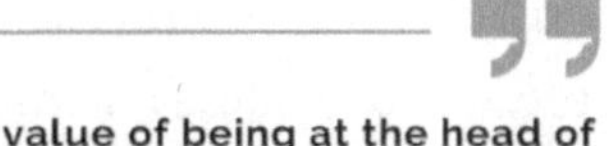

The value of being at the head of the organization is that it allows this leader to unify everybody to move in one common direction, not to compete with anyone for anything, but to empower each member no matter what role they play in the organization. The same unifying and empowering principles are employed in community engagements.

Someone possessing all the necessary competencies nowadays has been defined as a person who can combine knowledge, skills, and abilities. That's interesting because that's also supported by other experts in the leadership field. And that was what Nelson Mandela meant when he said that the real leader uses every issue, no matter how serious and sensitive, to ensure that, at the end of the debate, everybody emerges stronger and more united than ever before.

The value of being at the head of the organization is that it allows this leader to unify everybody to move in one common direction, not to compete with anyone for anything, but to empower each member no matter what role they play in the organization. The same unifying and empowering principles are employed in community engagements.

"It doesn't really matter what the core values are, as long as the entire organization commits to those core values. The most important thing in any large organization is alignment [around values and vision]," says Tony Hsieh of Zappos.

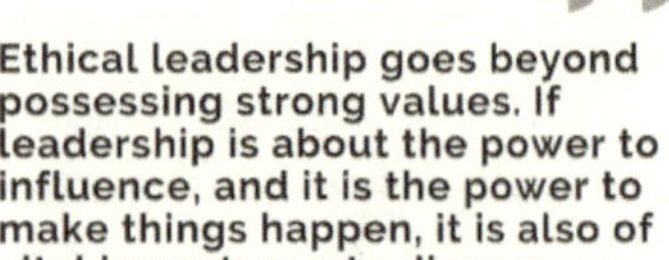

Ethical leadership goes beyond possessing strong values. If leadership is about the power to influence, and it is the power to make things happen, it is also of vital importance to discuss insights on how leadership should be perceived as coupled with integrity and ethics.

Ethical leadership, therefore, goes beyond possessing strong values. If leadership is about the power to influence, and it is the power to make things happen, it is also of vital importance to discuss insights on how leadership should be perceived as coupled with integrity and ethics.

Some genuine characteristics embody ethical leadership, and these are what I hope to give an account of in this chapter.

## A. Values, dignity, virtues, integrity

Ethical leadership has been defined by experts as the leadership that is directed by respect for ethical beliefs and values, and the dignity and rights of others. It is mainly concerned with moral development and virtuous behavior. As this chapter's primary theme, it is important that we know the context of ethical leadership, so that it will not overlook any wrongdoing.

According to David Mayer (2012), ethical leaders are role models who communicate the importance of ethical standards, hold their employees accountable to those standards, and— crucially— design environments in which others work and live that are conducive to ethical behavior. Leaders also transmit ethics by building benevolent relationships and teaching others how to think about ethical questions, empowering ethical behavior among employees, and growing future ethical leaders.

He adds the following leadership ideas:

1. Make ethics a clear priority for our leadership. Being an ethical leader means going beyond being a good person. Ethical leaders make ethics a clear and consistent part of leadership agendas, set standards, model appropriate behavior, and hold everyone accountable. They're honest, especially when the truth is difficult to share.

2. Make ethical culture a part of every personnel-related function in your organization. Leaders must work hard through hiring, training, and performance-management systems, to bring in the right employees and then help them learn and internalize the organization's underlying values, in large part by understanding what behaviors leaders do and do not reward.

3. Encourage, measure, and reward ethical leadership at multiple levels. Ethical leadership from the top is important—because it creates an

> environment in which lower-level ethical leaders can flourish—but ethical leadership at the supervisory level has a huge impact on followers' attitudes and behavior.

Max Bazerman (2020) proposes A New Model for Ethical Leadership (Harvard Business Review). Rather than try to follow a set of simple rules, leaders and managers seeking to be more ethical should focus on creating the most value for society. This utilitarian view, Bazerman argues, blends philosophical thought with business school pragmatism and can inform a wide variety of managerial decisions in areas including hiring, negotiations, and even time management.

Creating value requires that managers confront and overcome the cognitive barriers that prevent them from being as ethical as they would like to be. Just as we rely on intuitive and deliberative thinking, he says, we have parallel systems for ethical decision-making. He proposes strategies for engaging the deliberative one to make more ethical choices. Managers who care about the value they create can influence others throughout the organization by utilizing the norms and decision-making environment they create.

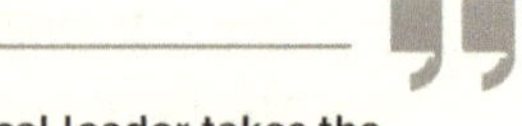

**An ethical leader takes the blame; a boss blames others. When a team fails, the leader believes that it's their responsibility to figure out what they did wrong before moving on to evaluating other people.**

## B. Ethical Leader versus Boss

Any community leader, manager, business or enterprise owner, or entrepreneur would tell us that a clear distinction exists between an ethical leader (in the truest sense of the word) and a boss.

Ethical leaders, according to Waida (2022), not only motivate and inspire their teams to perform their best, but are also part of the team themselves. They find a healthy balance between managing, leading, and jumping in to help when needed. They are also constantly researching new methods and ways to be a better leader.

A boss takes all the credit inside the organization space, compared to someone who sees leadership as a noble profession, where credit is shared by everybody.

An ethical leader takes the blame; a boss blames others. When a team fails, the leader believes that it's their responsibility to figure out what they did wrong before moving on to evaluating other people. They know that if a project didn't meet expectations, it may relate to the workplace culture, the systems they had already put in place or an oversight of theirs that can and should be corrected for the next project. Understanding the functions of management certainly helps too.

> Ethical leaders adopt a growth mindset. That means they are open to learning new ideas, hearing interesting takes from others, and are willing to try new things as they come up. This helps foster a more creative work environment for everyone. It also helps the entire team feel supported in the work they do, which leads to more productivity and better results.

The boss uses his power to put his name in the limelight. The ethical leader sees to it that fame and recognition are shared by the entire team. An ethical leader has an open mind. He knows that he does not know everything and wants to learn. A boss, on the other hand, already knows it all. And it is quite difficult to approach him about his mistakes and wrong decisions since he will not take any feedback well.

Ethical leaders adopt a growth mindset. That means they are open to learning new ideas, hearing interesting takes from others, and are willing to try new things as they come up. This helps foster a more creative work environment for everyone. It also helps the entire team feel supported in the work they do, which leads to more productivity and better results.

The ethical leader decides on utilitarianism, for the betterment of the entire organization. He collaborates, where a boss dictates. The ethical leader likes to work with other people to get the best positive results that the group is capable of. He doesn't simply rely on one or two managers to oversee progress. Although a good manager is a serious asset, ethical leaders are hands-on, brainstorming side by side with partners and employees on the team, to come up with innovative solutions.

> **An ethical leader sets an example; a boss makes an example out of people. Leaders make sure that the rules apply to them, too. They follow them, work them out, and make revisions as needed. They model the behavior they wish to see in the workplace. This often involves thinking positively, showing up early, and showing up when needed.**

An ethical leader empowers; a boss keeps a watchful eye. Leaders also set up systems and processes that make it easy for employees to make decisions on their own with minimal supervision. This can relate to finances, task management, and even customer relations. With proper communication, leaders make it easy for their team to have a certain level of autonomy, no matter what they're working on.

An ethical leader sets an example; a boss makes an example out of people. Leaders make sure that the rules apply to them, too. They follow them, work them out, and make revisions as needed. They model the behavior they wish to see in the workplace. This often involves thinking positively, showing up early, and showing up when needed.

## C. Emotional Well-being

Even at the core of our community engagements on a personal level, I believe that it's important to first look into improved emotional well-being, before any leadership task is undertaken. In the course of studying and practicing psychology, I have learned that emotional well-being and positive self-control gauge what could be one's future in ethical leadership.

No matter how toxic the environment becomes, end-of-the-line efficiency and productivity decrease if a person is not able to recognize the toxicity for what it is, look at it squarely in the eye, and do something to control it or prevent it from further spreading.

Workplace stress, unfortunately, prevails, sometimes unimpeded, in some workspaces. The study conducted by Bhui, et al. (2016) yielded the following results: Participants reported adverse working conditions and management practices as common causes of work stress. Stress-inducing management practices included unrealistic demands, lack of support, unfair treatment, low decision latitude, lack of appreciation, effort-reward imbalance, conflicting roles, lack of transparency, and poor communication. Organizational interventions were perceived as effective if they improved management styles, and included physical exercise, taking breaks, and ensuring adequate time for planning work tasks. Personal interventions used outside of work were important to prevent and remedy stress.

David Vallance, in his book *Workplace Stress is Eroding Our Productivity* (2019), claims that more than 90 percent of workers experience stress at work and almost a third say their stress is either high or unsustainably high. Skyrocketing stress levels are having detrimental macroeconomic effects with absenteeism rising and productivity falling.

Dr. Russell Thackeray describes stress as specific hormones the body uses to create the energy we need to live our lives.

"Stress becomes disruptive when our requests for energy begin to overwhelm us or when they combine with emotional cues that can trigger the fight-or-flight response," Thackery explains. "If we experience too many emotional and workload sources of stress, we begin to experience the challenge of cortisol. As it's a steroid hormone, the more that is produced, the more it begins to work against us and, in the long term, negatively affect our health."

When people become overwhelmed by stress, they can experience a debilitating salvo of cognitive and physical afflictions, including increased risk of heart disease, diabetes, fatigue, burnout, concentration problems, and depression.

While many people associate serious stress-related conditions with individuals in high-pressure roles, stress affects a wide range of people. And even people who experience mild or moderate stress are very susceptible to stress-induced health and performance problems, especially if they endure over a prolonged period.

## D. Open Communication

Shiv Sharma writes in *What is Open Communication and Why is it Important?* that open communication happens in a team when its members are empowered to share their thoughts without any fear of repercussions. It's not a one-off phenomenon. It's a cultural trait that teams cultivate with practice. Open communication helps build trust in the organization and sows the seeds of transforming employees into co-entrepreneurs.

Miscommunication starts from the littlest thing. Someone is not properly acknowledged, or one is talked about through the grapevine, or an important letter has been mislaid, etc. If small, no matter how trivial or petty they may seem, are not dealt with appropriately, in addition to being dealt with right away, things could get ugly, and a total communication breakdown could happen.

Dale Carnegie famously said, "I've never done any thinking about failure." This is the way problems in workplaces must be dealt with and resolved. Positive-thinking, forward-looking attitudes, empathy and sincerity, and collaboration will put to an end many of the skirmishes, conflicts, and arguments in our places of work.

> An ethical leader sets an example; a boss makes an example out of people. Leaders make sure that the rules apply to them, too. They follow them, work them out, and make revisions as needed. They model the behavior they wish to see in the workplace. This often involves thinking positively, showing up early, and showing up when needed.

The question now is, how do we evolve, and then internalize all these characteristics of ethical leadership (A, B, C, and D), so that at the end of each working day, the employees in the organization still go home emotionally healthy, sound, and fulfilled?

First, it is important to align our personal values with the vision and mission of the organization, and with the kind of people working there. Such simple ways as acknowledging the work of others and their contribution to the organization, and showing genuine gratitude, go a long way toward creating smooth and pleasant scenarios.

Learning to acknowledge and value gratitude are soft skills that the leader of the day must possess. If these are not innate characteristics, then there are ways to learn them, and eventually learning them will make a huge difference between exhibiting any style of leadership and exhibiting: ethical leadership.

Second, I believe that the organization should hire smart people. According to Steve Jobs, "It doesn't make sense to hire smart people and tell them what to do; we hire smart people so they can tell us what to do."

We should give employees the right environment for "thought sparks" that will initiate imagination and creativity, while still being true to individuality and expression. These thought sparks are "insightful ideas, actionable suggestions, strategic thinking and innovation", according to Rita McGrath of Columbia Business School. These could be "short, digestible courses that will give everyone in the organization the chance to learn the language and practices of innovation in a smart, easy-to-consume format."

This means that the ethical leader, after hiring the smart people, gives them enough room to do their jobs and be experts in their fields, without constantly breathing down their necks. In situations like these, the leader may very easily feel not in control anymore, jealous even, of the attention and rewards that the smart people get. The leader may even feel defiant, and, possibly, vengeful. But if the leader is truly ethical, he will consider being grateful to them as the moral thing and this quality is part of the integral makeup of good leadership.

Emotional maturity, self-control, and overall mental well-being would be applied here, especially during the leader's interaction with the people in the organization.

Ethical leaders walk the talk. When the signage says "Be prompt", "No smoking", and "No stealing", they should be the first ones to abide by what these signs say. If they violate any of them, then they could be the source of rumor-mongering and ill-will in the company. Distrust and skepticism eventually follow.

The leader clearly wants to be followed, and sometimes, people do hang on to his every word. However, it is never certain how his effect and influence will be received across different nationalities and varying ethnicities, which is how the modern workplace is described. Cultural relativity is always present, so much so that a bandwagon effect won't always work.

When I teach at university, I always make it a policy to never be late for my classes. I believe that I have set a perfectly straight record of no absences during these many years and thus have made myself an unquestionable role model for the trait of always coming in early. I have taught colleagues and students the wonders of this particular trait.

Each leader displays personal leadership styles and characteristics and these are commendable. I should add, however, that these styles should also be value-driven and value-laden for them to work, especially in highly diversified environments where people are constantly deeking role models for themselves to emulate.

The leader clearly wants to be followed, and sometimes, people do hang on to his every word. However, it is never certain how his effect and influence will be received across different nationalities and varying ethnicities, which is how the modern workplace is described. Cultural relativity is always present, so much so that a bandwagon effect won't always work.

Conventions, trends, customs, and patterns, putting people in the same areas, labeling them together as such, hurt and offend more often than they do the opposite. Ethical leadership, therefore, demands sensitivity, delicacy, and perceptiveness.

The spirit behind all of these, the synergy, so to speak, that inspires and ties everything together, is, I would say, one's personal strength to lead others, to care for others. It is vigor, stability, fortitude. It is a decision that one has to make if he wants to be an ethical leader.

I can say that this strength in itself is power, something that outsiders will have to contend with if they want a piece of the organization.

This strength, I believe, is innate and intrinsic, sometimes intuitive. It is not taught in schools (it cannot be taught at any learning institution), nor is it mastered in webinars, conferences, and short-term courses, much akin to watching a speaker talk about strength and the audience experience its raw form, even before leaving the room.

This strength is more than leadership or ethical style, much more than a demeanor or disposition. I believe that it is a gift from a Giver who has given it all. That would be my basic premise. This strength is received when one travels through life fearful and afraid at the beginning, but comes out fearless and daring and an absolute winner.

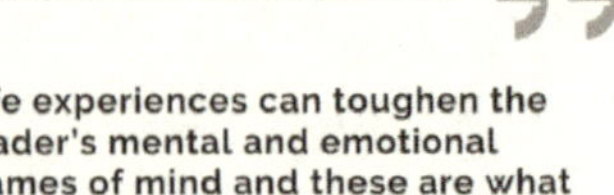

Life experiences can toughen the leader's mental and emotional frames of mind and these are what he intends to share with his colleagues. Although not everyone who dreams of becoming an ethical leader has had this kind of strength delivered to them, forged in the fire of life experience, this is the place where true, unerring, and faithful ethical leadership springs from.

Only a tough endurance of pain could birth this kind of strength, this ethical leadership style that comes from the inner core and is transmitted to others because the leader knows how it feels to be left alone, disregarded, feeling both shame and guilt, and without any resource to hold body and soul together.

All these life experiences can toughen the leader's mental and emotional frames of mind and these are what he intends to share with his colleagues. Although not everyone who dreams of becoming an ethical leader has had this kind of strength delivered to them, forged in the fire of life experience, this is the place where true, unerring, and faithful ethical leadership springs from.

And this is a good place to start.

## Reflections

Key Insights: Draw from this Chapter your major takeaways.

1. ______________________________

______________________________

______________________________

2. ______________________________

______________________________

______________________________

3. ______________________________

______________________________

______________________________

Recount events in your life related to the Key Insights.

1. ______________________________

______________________________

______________________________

2. ______________________________

______________________________

______________________________

3. ______________________________

______________________________

______________________________

How can these Key Insights guide you and prepare you for life's present and future challenges?

1. ______________________________________________

______________________________________________

______________________________________________

2. ______________________________________________

______________________________________________

______________________________________________

3. ______________________________________________

______________________________________________

______________________________________________

## Chapter 12

# A Journey to Happiness

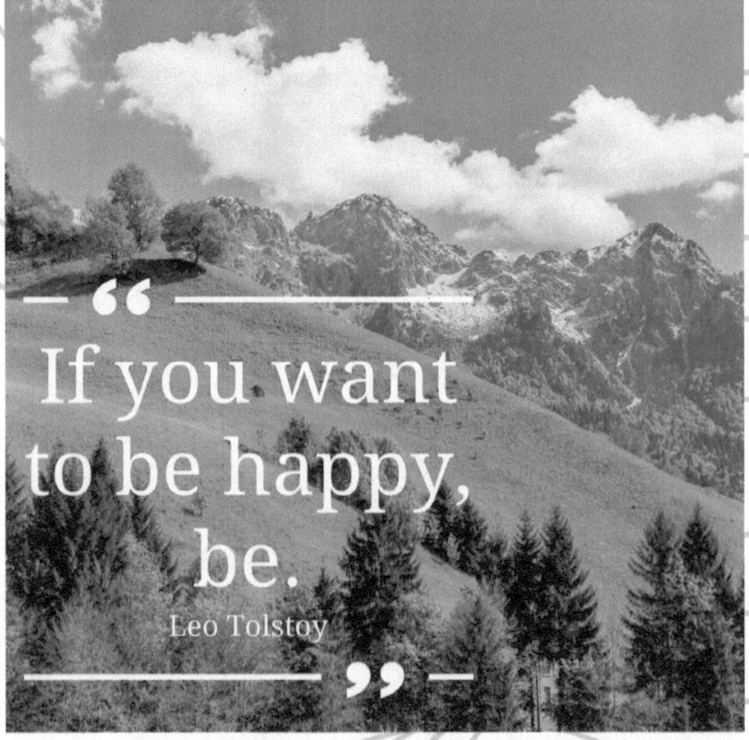
"
If you want
to be happy,
be.
Leo Tolstoy
"

# How Happy is the Little Stone

*Emily Dickinson*

How happy is the little Stone
That rambles in the Road alone,
And doesn't care about Careers
And Exigencies never fears --
Whose Coat of elemental Brown
A passing Universe put on,
And independent as the Sun
Associates or glows alone,
Fulfilling absolute Decree
In casual simplicity.

And so my tale has reached to a close.

Like everything else, my story – at least, up until this point – has reached its end. Deep gratitude has overwhelmed me because, in a few pages, I was able to tell you, dear Reader, the story of my life. It is my sincerest wish that you were able to see your own stories reflected therein and you were able to distill lessons from mine, and received some help and instruction for you to get by and move forward with confidence.

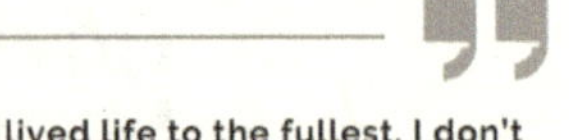

I have lived life to the fullest. I don't have any regrets. I know that every event that happened, happened for a reason. I grew up, I learned, I acquired, I absorbed, I gained, I witnessed, and I continue to do so – after all, life is far from over!

I have but a few more things to tell you, and then I am done with my task.

Just like anyone else's life, mine isn't perfect. I went through my primary years living the life of a stuttering, acutely shy young boy. I have had my fair share of humiliation from classmates and grown-ups alike, even from people who should have known better, some carers and teachers.

This book, from its initial pages to these lines that you are reading now, dear Reader, is a testament to the kind of life that I lived – and left. I outgrew my early life, that way of thinking, that mode of being. I decided that, once and for all, there would no longer be an "active inside, passive outside," dichotomy for me, that it was high time I show people, prove to them, in fact, that I could overcome my natural shyness, stand up, that I could look people in the eye, evaluate what they were saying, appreciate them, and confidently say my piece in return.

I have lived life to the fullest. I don't have any regrets. I know that every event that happened, happened for a reason. I grew up, I learned, I acquired, I absorbed, I gained, I witnessed, and I continue to do so – after all, life is far from over!

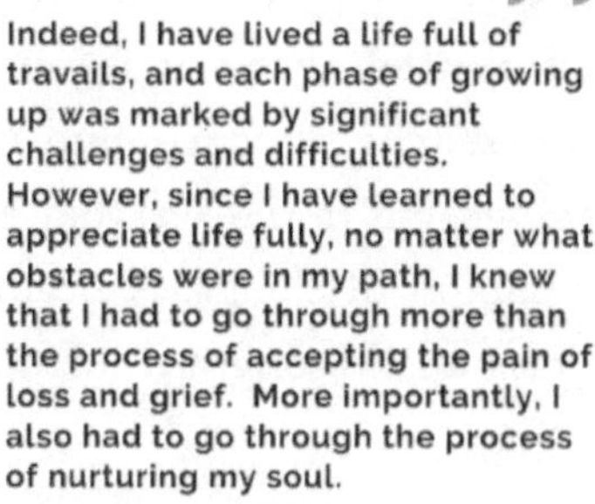
Indeed, I have lived a life full of travails, and each phase of growing up was marked by significant challenges and difficulties. However, since I have learned to appreciate life fully, no matter what obstacles were in my path, I knew that I had to go through more than the process of accepting the pain of loss and grief. More importantly, I also had to go through the process of nurturing my soul.

What more is there to ask for? Every little task, each disappointment made me the kind of person that I am now.

Indeed, I have lived a life full of travails, and each phase of growing up was marked by significant challenges and difficulties. However, since I have learned to appreciate life fully, no matter what obstacles were in my path, I knew that I had to go through more than the process of accepting the pain of loss and grief. More importantly, I also had to go through the process of nurturing my soul.

I've always known the necessity of cultivating my own happiness, and even at a tender age, I decided that I would be happy. No matter what my circumstances were, it was my decision that I would be happy. Once I made the decision, I tried to look for happiness even in the most mundane of things, and, in so doing, I found a true sense of joy, a certain peace.

Dear Reader, you may also want to follow my example and do this. Search for happiness in the simple things. More often than not, it can be found right under our very noses. It is seldom found in the great, grand scheme of things, but in the everyday, in the most ordinary, the most common of things. A beautiful stone, dew on the green grass, an old song, a child's gaze – all of these are wondrous things.

I knew, too, even at a tender age, that happiness must be shared for me to be able to truly experience it. It was not possible to simply keep it to myself. It was meant to be shared with people who, like me, were destined to be happy. My sense of happiness is shared in a cyclical sort of way. Blessing upon blessing, laughter upon laughter, happiness upon happiness. In the end, I saw that I had been made a vessel of joy for others to emulate.

This happiness, once found, must be nurtured. We must care for it, it must be tendered constantly, watered, and fed, the way we care for someone whom we love very deeply. Otherwise, it will escape or will be trampled underfoot, and we won't know anymore the feeling of how to be happy again.

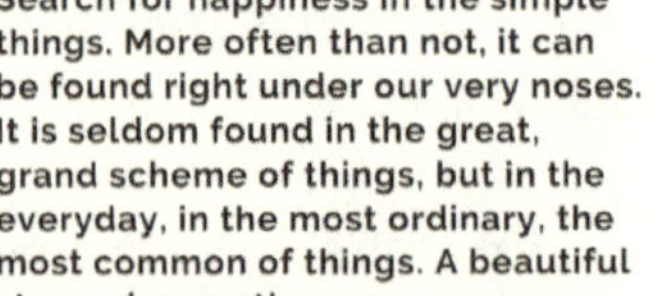

Nurturing our happiness should start from the beginning. I believe that genuinely happy people are destined to be happy and they aim to make others equally happy. Our families were overjoyed to witness our arrival into the world. Our little cries and our little coos brought laughter to the household. We did not realize it, but even as little tots, we were already vessels of comfort and joy.

I'm happy to see my son Adler grow up as a loving person and fulfill his destiny of being a vessel of happiness himself. I am content with my work, my engagements, my obligations – all these make me happy. My community encounters through our mental health programs create happiness for me and my team. My scholarship program for meritorious college students makes me happy. A sense of awe, of deep emotion, prevails, of being there, of having arrived and completed in full circle a very long, wearying, journey. Mhel, Romel, and Cris – my best friends for life, nudge me gently towards positivity whenever I see the gloom of this dark world.

My heart is full. Having published my first book during the height of the pandemic, I saw it as a manifold blessing from God. That first book was the product of deep reflective thinking while I myself was ill with coronavirus and with diabetes. That reflective thinking extended to this,

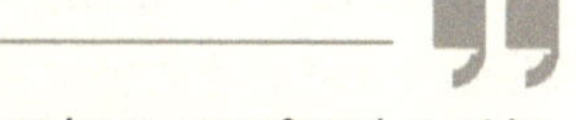

**This happiness, once found, must be nurtured. We must care for it, it must be tendered constantly, watered, and fed, the way we care for someone whom we love very deeply. Otherwise, it will escape or will be trampled underfoot, and we won't know anymore the feeling of how to be happy again.**

my second book. I am overflowing with gratitude and happiness.

I asked myself: what are people's sources of happiness? Is it beneficial for one to be happy? Are there strategies for happiness that we can probably apply and share?

Positive psychology and so as the philosophers of ancient times tell us that happiness is a choice. If it is, then it is a frame of mind, more than of emotions. It is a state of well-being that encompasses living a good life with a sense of meaning and deep commitment and therefore goes beyond contentment.

The concept of happiness is the cornerstone of the assumptions of positive psychology. Happiness is characterized by the experience of more frequent, positive, and affective conditions than negative ones, as well as the perception that one is progressing toward important life goals (Tkach & Lyubomirsky, 2006).

Identifying factors that contribute to happiness has proven to be challenging. Interestingly, though, one thing that does stand out in the research to date is that the attainment and pursuit of pleasure and gratification may not always lead to happiness.

Certain kinds of environmental factors or conditions are associated with happiness and include such external factors as individual income, labor market status, health, family, social relationships, moral values, and many others (Carr, 2004; Selim, 2008; Diener, Oishi & Lucas, 2003).

For internal factors, psychological well-being includes a sense of control or autonomy, feelings of meaning and purpose, personal expressiveness, feelings of belongingness, social contribution, competence, personal growth, and self-acceptance (Maddox, 2020).

An individual with an improved immune system can more easily handle various types of stresses and, therefore, certain kinds of mental illnesses since they emit feelings of hope, positivity, belongingness, and fulfillment.

This pursuit of happiness, moreover, is both personal and global, since the cornerstone of happiness is more concerned with the desired personal outcomes, which may vary across individuals. It pertains to the quality of our contentment with the people with whom we interact.

Our personal definition of happiness is, more often than not, based on the feelings that we are indeed happy. And for some, on a professional note, it means landing good jobs and being financially free and being able to support, as well as being supportive of families. Others may equate happiness with their positions in their organizations, from where their power and prestige emanate.

This pursuit of happiness, moreover, is both personal and global, since the cornerstone of happiness is more concerned with the desired personal outcomes, which may vary across individuals. It pertains to the quality of our contentment with the people with whom we interact.

Hence, looking back on the reflective state that most of us went through during the more than two-year pandemic, we have learned many, many insights and have reached new understandings.

Firstly, we learned that money cannot buy happiness, nor can it guarantee security, safety, and wellness. All we can do – and indeed, we cannot do anything else but this – is to be content with what we *do* have.

It is useless for us to lament over lost opportunities, lost chances. They have come and gone. Thompson (2020) describes the young people who missed opportunities during the pandemic as 'Generation Corona', who are also grieving lost moments. "In addition to lost career and education opportunities, the pandemic has robbed many young people of the chance to mark and celebrate big milestones in their young lives: high school graduations, proms and university graduation ceremonies, even milestone birthdays."

> **During the pandemic, when we saw millions dying, even while countries desperately tried to contain the virus, we came to appreciate family like never before. Every family member is now our treasure. Others consider their families their entire universe, everything else is secondary. That job is secondary, that promotion is secondary, that preferment is secondary. Nothing can take the place of the family and those shared values that kept us bound to one another, even while morale was at rock bottom, because of unprecedented grief and loss.**

According to Professor Heather Servaty-Seib of Purdue University, missed moments should have provided an important centering point, a point of reflection, a point of community around an experience that is being lost. The absence of such moments takes away a sense of community and collective celebration around an individual moving from one state of being or one place to another.

Secondly, during the pandemic, when we saw millions dying, even while countries desperately tried to contain the virus, we came to appreciate family like never before. Every family member is now our treasure. Others consider their families their entire universe, everything else is secondary. That job is secondary, that promotion is secondary, that preferment is secondary. Nothing can take the place of the family and those shared values that kept us bound to one another, even while morale was at rock bottom, because of unprecedented grief and loss.

As a result the family has sprung into the very center of the concept of happiness and we try ways to nurture family since our very happiness depends on it.

The family is one of the building blocks of society, and so its structure and role reflect social changes. According to Dee Marques (2022), over the past thirty years, the traditional family unit has evolved significantly. Right now there isn't a single concept of family that applies universally. Blood families and tribal families co-exist with one another. Although the family structure may have changed, its importance has not.

One of the reasons why family is necessary for happiness is because it usually provides financial stability in our early years. Having our basic needs covered is crucial when it comes to setting the basis for a happy life.

Studies show, however, that the link between family and happiness extends beyond money or possessions. It cannot be equated with wealth or being famous or having one's dream job. These are myths and misconceptions, and cannot be made baselines for happiness.

Researchers followed up hundreds of families for a decade and found that the quality of family bonds mattered more to overall happiness than income (Sharp, 2015).

Support is one of the reasons why family is important for happiness. And this support goes both ways: according to a study, nearly 70 percent of parents depend on their children for emotional support. Research also shows that knowing someone has your back can counter stress, depressive symptoms, and low self-esteem in young people.

Happiness is not simply feeling good. It comes with a proper set of values that must be developed for that family to thrive. Self-compassion, as explained in the previous chapter, is foremost. Mindfulness, optimism, and resilience all prove to be equally worthy in equipping members of the family in dealing with everyday struggles and stress. Kindness, compassion, altruism, simplicity, humility, and helpfulness all work towards achieving a more ideal family life.

Thirdly, holding on to grudges and regrets because of mistakes made in the past will surely make us *un*happy. We don't necessarily have to live in the past. It cannot be brought back anyway. A happy person is hopeful and positive about the future and is forward-looking.

Iterative positive psychology is that branch of psychology that explores human welfare and investigates flourishing advancements, such as highlighting the importance of practicing optimism and its impact on lasting human relations. Studied are ways of nurturing ourselves so that we can experience positive emotions and develop authentic relationships while building meaningful lives.

Holding on to grudges and regrets because of mistakes made in the past will surely make us unhappy. We don't necessarily have to live in the past. It cannot be brought back anyway. A happy person is hopeful and positive about the future and is forward-looking.

According to Lomas et al. (2019), as positive psychology has developed as a field, questions have arisen around how to ensure best practice, including respect for ethics. The field lacks clear ethical guidelines that will assist practitioners in their studies of happiness.

Aiming to address this gap, the authors have devised a set of guidelines, in collaboration with key stakeholders across the positive psychology community, published in the International Journal of Wellbeing. The authors summarize the importance, development, content, and future directions of these "happiness" guidelines, thus providing a concise overview of this important project. It is hoped that the guidelines will not only highlight the importance of ethical practice but offer practical suggestions for guiding practitioners in the field concerning human happiness and well-being.

Fourthly, the overarching principle is the essence of self-determined happiness. Cherry (2019) discusses self-determination as an important concept that refers to each person's ability to make choices and manage their own life. This ability plays an important role in psychological health and well-being. Self-determination allows people to feel that they have control over their choices and lives. It also has an impact on motivation—people feel more motivated to take action when they feel that what they do will affect the outcome.

This matters since we are the ones setting our boundaries, creating the criteria for our own happiness. It is, indeed, a bumpy road, since self-determined happiness means quantifying happiness, something which is rarely, if ever, possible. Happiness is thoroughly subjective, differing from one person to the next. The reasons for the happiness of one person may be drastically different from the reasons of another.

Through the self-determination theory, we can help understand the things that might motivate our behaviors. Being self-determined, the autonomy and freedom to make choices that shape our destinies are important for each person's well-being. When we pursue intrinsically motivated things that are aligned with our goals, we feel happier and more capable of making good choices.

Self-determination includes self-choice and self-empowerment, being proactive in our choices of being happy. To arrive at that blissful state may not necessarily be dependent on the event or the activity, but on the brain that we were born with.

One of the benefits of happiness is a long life. Happy people tend to live longer because, according to science, the brain is basically powered up by certain electro-mechanical impulses that cause feelings of bliss.

According to Seladi-Schulman (2018), in her article *What Part of the Brain Controls Emotions?*, "imaging studies suggest that the happiness response originates partly in the limbic cortex. Another area called the precuneus also plays a role. The precuneus is involved in retrieving memories, maintaining our sense of self, and focusing our attention as we move about in our environment. People with larger gray matter volume in their right precuneus reported being happier. Experts think the precuneus processes certain information and converts it into feelings of happiness. For example, imagine you've spent a wonderful night out with someone you care about. When you recall this experience and others like it, you may experience a feeling of happiness."

> **I don't think that negative people appreciate the kind of sentimentality that comes with true giving from a generous heart. Social media may be a source of both stress and happiness, depending on what one intends to upload there for the world to see. Values and integrity play a major role in the determination of what to upload and what to withhold.**

Fifthly, authentic sources of happiness, as I see them, always begin with self-choice and end with self-actualization. Self-actualization represents a concept derived from humanistic psychological theory and, specifically, from the theory created by Abraham Maslow. Self-actualization, according to Maslow, represents the growth of an individual toward fulfillment of the highest needs—those for meaning in life, in particular. He created a psychological hierarchy of needs, the fulfillment of which theoretically leads to a culmination of the fulfillment of "being values," or the needs that are on the highest level of this hierarchy, representing meaning.

For self-actualization to be planted and for it to thrive, a good, fertile ground is needed. Practicality now supersedes mere concept. A high-paying job needed to support the self and family and anyone else who matters would be a good example of this. It was a happy thing that I was able to provide for the studies of my siblings at the universities where they chose to study and I consider it a great privilege to be the primary earner for my family. Today, I can send poor but praiseworthy students to school out of my earnings and I am grateful that I have done so for many years. I know that generosity is one of my purposes in life.

> Mindfulness can help us cope with depression, boost our psychological well-being, manage physical pain, and even provide us with good memory. When it comes to the way we think and feel, being mindful of our emotions helps us to switch to more positive mindsets and work towards being a 'better'—or at least, a happier—person.

I don't think that negative people appreciate the kind of sentimentality that comes with true giving from a generous heart. Social media may be a source of both stress and happiness, depending on what one intends to upload there for the world to see. Values and integrity play a major role in the determination of what to upload and what to withhold.

Happiness leads to optimism, believing that we can do things no matter how difficult these may seem to be, and hoping and doing our best to be able to do such things, thus making ourselves and others happy in the long run.

Finally, mindfulness of things can be another source of happiness. According to the American Psychological Association (APA.org, 2012), mindfulness is "...a moment-to-moment awareness of one's experience without judgment. In this sense, mindfulness is a state and not a trait. While it might be promoted by certain practices or activities, such as meditation, it is not equivalent to or synonymous with them." It involves awareness, and impartiality about what we gain from this awareness. In an age of social media, where opinions, likes, and commentary are more than forthcoming, it's easy to see how non-judgmental reflection can be a welcome change.

Daniel J. Siegel describes mindfulness "in its most general sense about waking up from a life on automatic, and being sensitive to novelty in our everyday experiences. ... Instead of being on automatic and mindless, mindfulness helps us awaken, and by reflecting on the mind we are enabled to make choices and thus change becomes possible" (Hampton, 2014).

Mindfulness can help us cope with depression, boost our psychological well-being, manage physical pain, and even provide us with good memory. When it comes to the way we think and feel, being mindful of our emotions helps us to switch to more positive mindsets and work towards being a 'better'—or at least, a happier—person.

Again, no one can strive to live a perfect life. Everyone is lacking or has suffered a loss in some way. This idea of wanting a perfect life derails us from being happy (i.e. it blocks the path towards happiness).

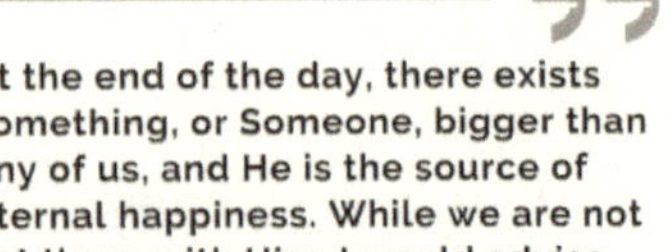

> **At the end of the day, there exists something, or Someone, bigger than any of us, and He is the source of eternal happiness. While we are not yet there with Him, I would advise each one of us to appreciate life, live life to its full. Perhaps each time we gain mastery of our negative emotions and instead make room for the happy ones, one soul will have been saved.**

One must also believe, however, that these are not stumbling blocks. These are mere stepping stones towards learning the ups and downs of life and believing the lessons that go with them.

Let us not be too hard on ourselves, nor expect too much from others. We cannot change the past. We must forgive and then let go. Let us cultivate something fresh, new, and different. Let us cultivate compassion, love, and laughter. These are gateways to happiness.

> **As we equip ourselves with our life lessons, our own stories, and our competencies, we inspire others by continuously igniting the passion to serve and kindling the desire to look for what is true, and what is right and what is best in humanity.**

At the end of the day, there exists something, or Someone, bigger than any of us, and He is the source of eternal happiness. While we are not yet there with Him, I would advise each one of us to appreciate life, live life to its full. Perhaps each time we gain mastery of our negative emotions and instead make room for the happy ones, one soul will have been saved.

Our journey to finding ourselves and our own happiness will have thus begun.

In the long run, self-discovery and growth, no matter how painful they are, create a powerful force that contributes to the betterment of ourselves and thus the betterment of the communities we serve.

As we equip ourselves with our life lessons, our own stories, and our competencies, we inspire others by continuously igniting the passion to serve and kindling the desire to look for what is true, and what is right and what is best in humanity.

Yes, we are imperfect. We are often disheartened, disappointed, bruised. We are often distressed due to the seemingly insurmountable waves of struggle and adversity.

But, dear Reader, we are Unbroken.

And Unbroken we shall remain.

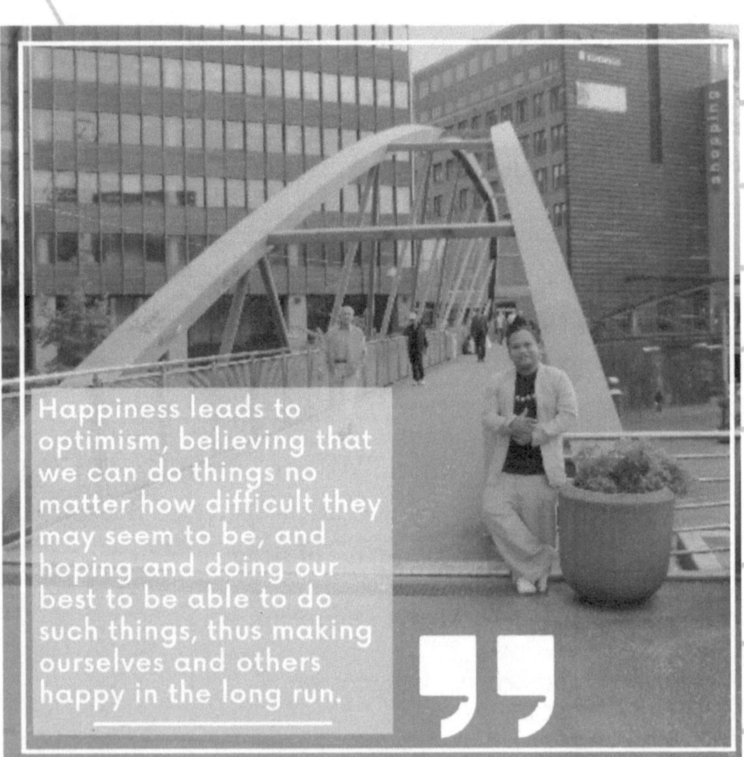
Happiness leads to optimism, believing that we can do things no matter how difficult they may seem to be, and hoping and doing our best to be able to do such things, thus making ourselves and others happy in the long run.

## Reflections

Key Insights: Draw from this Chapter your major takeaways.

1. ______________________________

______________________________

______________________________

2. ______________________________

______________________________

______________________________

3. ______________________________

______________________________

______________________________

Recount events in your life related to the Key Insights.

1. ______________________________

______________________________

______________________________

2. ______________________________

______________________________

______________________________

3. ______________________________

______________________________

______________________________

How can these Key Insights guide you and prepare you for life's present and future challenges?

1. ______________________________

______________________________

______________________________

2. ______________________________

______________________________

______________________________

3. ______________________________

______________________________

______________________________

# References

American Psychological Association (2012). Stress in America: Impact of stress. https://www.apa.org/news/press/releases/stress/2012/impact

Askin, N., & Petriglieri, G. (August 26, 2016). Tony Hsieh at Zappos: Structure, culture and radical change. Harvard Business Review. https://store.hbr.org/product/tony-hsieh-at-zappos-structure-culture-and-radical-change/IN1249

Bailey, H. (July 28, 2021). The depression pendulum that swings back and forth. https://themighty.com/2021/07/depression-pendulum-perspective/

Bazerman, M. (September-October, 2020). A new model for ethical leadership. Harvard Business Review. https://hbr.org/2020/09/a-new-model-for-ethical-leadership

Bisharat, J. (September 12, 2019). Six mental shifts to reduce stress – and make you happier. https://medium.com/swlh/mental-shifts-to-reduce-your-stress-and-make-you-happier-63136993ef62

Carr, A. (2004). Positive Psychology: The science of happiness and human strength. New York: Bruner-Routledge.

Cherry, K. (March 15, 2021). Self-determination, theory and motivation. https://www.verywellmind.com/what-is-self-determination-theory-2795387

Choncé, M. (September 30, 2020). How to work the 7 scientific happiness factors into your daily routine. https://www.calendar.com/blog/7-scientific-happiness-factors/

Council of Europe. (2015). United Nations Sustainable Development Goals and Agenda 2030. https://www.coe.int/en/web/programmes/un-2030-agenda

Diener, E., Oishi, S., & Lucas, R. E. (2003). Personality, culture, and subjective well-being: Emotional and cognitive evaluations of life. Annual Review of Psychology, 54, 403-425. http://dx.doi.org/10.1146/annurev.psych.54.101601.145056

Ericson, J. (October 10, 2013). Is pessimism genetic? Research shows your outlook might be cloudy by genetic design. Medical Daily. https://www.medicaldaily.com/pessimism-genetic-research-shows-your-outlook-might-be-cloudy-genetic-design-259573

Forrest & Hanson (Hosts). (June 13, 2021). Fierce self-compassion with Dr. Kristin Neff. https://self-compassion.org/fierce-self-compassion/https://doi.org/10.1007/s10902-005-4754-1

Illsley-Clarke, J. (2022). Words that help: Affirmations for any age. In Developmental Affirmations. The University of Minnesota Extension. https://extension.umn.edu/overindulgence/developmental-affirmations

Kauffman, R. (2016). Psychology of survival. Frostburg State University. https://www.frostburg.edu/faculty/rkauffman/_files/images_preppers_chapters/Ch02-Psychology_v2.pdf

Kramler, K. (2004). Surviving the extremes: A doctor's journey to the limits of human endurance. New York: St. Martin's Press. https://www.amazon.com/Surviving-Extremes-Doctors-Journey-Endurance-ebook/dp/B000FC0YTU

Lomas, T., et al. (2019). Developing ethical guidelines for Positive Psychology Practice: An ongoing, iterative, collaborative endeavor. The Journal of Positive Psychology, 15(8), 1-6. https://www.tandfonline.com/doi/abs/10.1080/17439760.2019.1651892

Luenondonk, M. (July 25, 2020). Transformational leadership guide: Definition, qualities, pros & cons, examples. https://www.cleverism.com/transformational-leadership-guide/

Marsh, J. (2013). Empathy and the greater good. https://greatergood.berkeley.edu/video/item/empathy_and_the_greater_good

Mayer, D., et al. (2012). Who displays ethical leadership, and why does it matter? An examination of antecedents and consequences of ethical leadership. The Academy of Management Journal, 55(1), 151-171. https://journals.aom.org/doi/10.5465/amj.2008.0276

McGrath, R. (September 22, 2016). Constantly reconfiguring and adapting your business. Columbia Business School. https://www.youtube.com/watch?v=DVVfgHZdV60

Nolen, J. (2017). Learned helplessness. https://www.britannica.com/science/learned-helplessness

Roncero, A. (June 21, 2021). Automatic negative thoughts: How to identify and fix them. https://www.betterup.com/blog/automatic-thoughts

San Luis, G. (July 6, 2022). Is ethical leadership still relevant today? https://business.inquirer.net/325236/is-ethical-leadership-still-relevant-today

Sandoui, A. (March 23, 2018). Why self-love is important and how to cultivate it. https://www.medicalnewstoday.com/articles/321309

Scott, E. (October 11, 2020). What is optimism? https://www.verywellmind.com/the-benefits-of-optimism-3144811

Seladi-Schulman, J. (July 23, 2018). What part of the brain controls emotions? https://www.healthline.com/health/what-part-of-the-brain-controls-emotions#:~:text=The%20limbic%20system%20is%20a,for%20behavioral%20and%20emotional%20responses

Selim, S. (2008). Life satisfaction and happiness in Turkey. Social Indicators Research, 88, 531–562. http://dx.doi.org/10.1007/s11205-007-9218-z

Servaty-Seib, H. & Hamilton, L. (2006). Educational performance and persistence of bereaved college students. Journal of College Student Development, 47(2), 225-234. https://scholar.google.com/citations?view_op=view_citation&hl=en&user=f4EdOLIAAAAJ&citation_for_view=f4EdOLIAAAAJ:d1gkVwhDpl0C

Sharma, R. (August 5, 2019). Authentic leadership. https://managemagazine.com/article-bank/leadership/robin-sharma-authentic-leadership/

Sharma, S. (n.d.) What is open communication and why is it important? https://taskworld.com/blog/what-is-open-communication-and-why-is-it-important/

Sharp, T. (2015). The happiness handbook. Finch Publishing. https://www.amazon.com/Happiness-Handbook-Dr-Timothy-Sharp/dp/1925048063

Sherwood, B. (2009). The survivor's club: The secrets and science that could save your life. New York: Grand Central Publishing. https://archive.org/details/survivorsclubsec00sher

Siegel, D. (August 26, 2015). The science of mindfulness. https://www.youtube.com/watch?v=aPlG_w40qOE

Thackeray, Russell (November 14, 2020). Getting stress into perspective. https://www.youtube.com/watch?v=HSOzdTTL2ec

Tkach, C., & Lyubomirsky, S. (2006). How do people pursue happiness?: Relating personality, happiness-increasing strategies, and well-being. Journal of Happiness Studies: An Interdisciplinary Forum on Subjective Well-Being, 7(2), 183–225. https://psycnet.apa.org/record/2006-09600-004

Tripathy, M. (2019). The power of ethics: Rethinking leadership roles at workplaces. Multidisciplinary Journal of Education, Social and Technological Sciences, 6(2), 134. https://www.researchgate.net/publication/336249850_The_Power_of_Ethics_Rethinking_Leadership_Roles_at_Workplaces

Vallance, D. (July 24, 2019). Workplace stress is eroding our productivity. https://blog.dropbox.com/topics/work-culture/stress-making-productivity-worse

Waida, M. (June 3, 2022). Boss versus leader: What is the difference? https://www.wrike.com/blog/boss-vs-leader-infographic/

# Reach Out

Engage. Collaborate. Reach out.

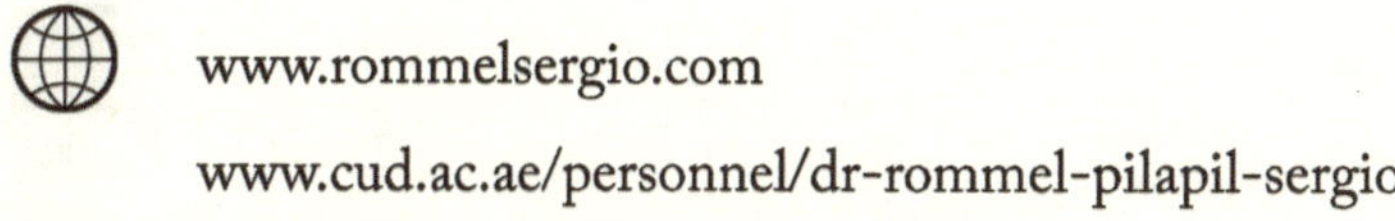

www.rommelsergio.com

www.cud.ac.ae/personnel/dr-rommel-pilapil-sergio

www.facebook.com/rommel.p.sergio

www.linkedin.com/in/rommelsergiophd/

www.instagram.com/sergio_travelteleporter/

www.twitter.com/iamrommelsergio

tiktok.com/@iamrommelsergio

email@rommelsergio.com

# About the Author

Rommel Sergio, PhD is a community leader, a multi-award winning educator, Amazon best selling author, and distinguished academic.

A humanitarian at heart, Dr. Rommel has been spearheading pro bono counseling programs for distressed overseas workers in the United Arab Emirates (UAE). Moreover, he has extended free educational consulting in selected schools in Dubai, UAE through psychosocial services, HR, and organizational development.

He has both founded the Psychological Society of the Philippines-Dubai Chapter and has served on the Founding Board of the same organization in the UAE. He has supported free online counseling for the community in the Philippines, Middle East, and Europe during the pandemic.

His over thirty years of experience as a community leader has enabled him to establish numerous mental health programs in various schools in the UAE. He has implemented psychosocial initiatives for community leaders and educators in the Middle East and the Philippines.

As a philanthropist, he has established the Dr. Rommel Sergio Scholarship Foundation to support the underprivileged college students. His groundbreaking research on emotional intelligence, organizational and personal wellness, leadership, and mental health spurred him to write his first book, *Management Cases: Thriving Organizations in the New Normal*, an Amazon best-seller.

Prior to more than 20 years of teaching on both undergraduate and graduate programs, Dr. Rommel served as HR Director and as Organizational Development Consultant with various organizations in the UAE and the Philippines.

He is currently Associate Dean and a Professor of Management at Canadian University Dubai, UAE.

www.ingramcontent.com/pod-product-compliance
Lightning Source LLC
LaVergne TN
LVHW041200150826
845673LV00001B/240

*9798887835921*